GOD SPEAKS AS

HIS

SPIRIT EMPOWERS

ANTHONY A EDDY

Front Cover Art

'The Approaching Storm'— G 'Lucré' Bauerfeind (2008)

Cover Photography by AA Eddy

This photographic image is approved by and used

with the artist's kind permission granted in 2011

Original Oil on Canvas

100cms x 79cms (39.4in x 31.1in)

in possession of A A Eddy

GOD Speaks as His

Of that which should become of imminent concern to man:
the time for his preparation is coming to an end—
bringing a dilemma before the mindset of man;
a course of action to be under urgency,
action which saves an errant life.

Spirit Empowers

For herein is the need explained in detail:
laid bare for the assimilation of man;
declared in intensity of purpose
for the noticing of man
before it is too late.

Anthony A Eddy
(Scribe)

Copyright and Publishing

© 2019 by BookWhip Publishing.

All rights reserved. No part of this publication may be reproduced, stored in a retrieval system or transmitted in any way by any means, electronic, mechanical, photocopy, recording or otherwise without the prior permission of the author except as provided by USA copyright law.

Printed in the United States of America

Soft Cover ISBN: 978-1-950580-90-3
Hard Cover ISBN: 978-1-951469-53-5
Ebook ISBN: 978-1-951469-54-2

3. "GOD Speaks as His Spirit Empowers"

Cover design, Manuscript Content and Layout, Conceptual Related Imagery and titling texts, ©® Copyright 2010, 2012, 2015, 2017, 2018, 2019 by The Advent Charitable Trust, CC45056, Hamilton, New Zealand. All rights reserved worldwide.

www.thewebsiteofthelord.org.nz

Prepared on a 27in iMac™© with the use of Nisus®© Writer Pro. All trademarks™ and intellectual rights remain the property of their respective owners.

To order additional copies of this book, contact:
Bookwhip
1-855-339-3589
https://www.bookwhip.com

Dedication

I again have very real cause for gratitude in offering the preparation of this, His third, book also into His care.

*To our God of love, of justice, of redemption
who is very interested in all we do
and in our achieving our return home.*

For He alone is worthy of the devotion of Man.

*All funds received go in their entirety
to
The Advent Charitable Trust
in order to further,
unless directed by a donor,
the scope and the objectives
of
this Charity's Christian Call
within
The Kingdom of God.*

The Scribe
The Advent Charitable Trust
Hamilton, New Zealand

The Parts of The End-time Psalms of God are—

	Pages	Total Words
1. GOD Speaks of Return and Bannered	418	87,061
2. GOD Speaks to Man on The Internet	498	122,349
3. GOD Speaks as His Spirit Empowers	272	68,187
4. GOD Speaks to Man in The End-time	248	62,358
5. GOD Speaks in Letters of Eternity	202	48,193
6. GOD Speaks to His Bridal Presence	326	78,183
7. GOD Speaks to His Edifice	512	122,516
8. GOD Speaks of Loving His Creation	280	67,234
9. GOD Speaks Now of a Seal Revealed	124	25,485

Acknowledgements

My very special thanks and appreciation both to my Pastor, and also in his callings both as a prophet and an apostle, and to his wife. They always welcomed us into their home both for teaching and for social occasions. Prior to the completion of this third book of The Lord's Website's scrolls, they have departed, after 21 years, in furtherance of a call to another area of New Zealand.

Without his support, counsel and encouragement, sometimes with a silent glance, this receipt of divine leadings would not have so easily come to be.

The items, as they have been received, have been handed regularly to him up until his departure for his calling relocation in December 2010. Our fellowship's leadership have since been kept informed.

May God our loving Father, Jesus Christ His Son, together with The Holy Spirit as our counsellor— bless and favour his family in all they do and bring to pass in the growth and development of His Kingdom here in New Zealand and around the world.

The Banner of The Kingdom was first flown as a Flag at
10.30am on Monday, 1st September 2008
in Hamilton, New Zealand.

The Banner of The Kingdom was first flown as a Flag on His Church in India in the village of **Burripalem**
near Tenali, Andhra Pradesh
on
Sunday, 31st July 2011
in unity with
Reaching Forward Ministries, Tenali, Andhra Pradesh, India.

Prelude

This, His third book within a trilogy— which very quickly became part of a greater work— still speaks of the urgency attending the need for preparation: the urgency for awareness of the coming storm; the urgency of seeking the Kingdom of God— of Jesus The Messiah— while it is today. May a sense of urgency propel the seekers into a destiny within the presence of The King.

Agapé,
Anthony,
His servant and His scribe.

Contents— Order Received

DI Divine Intent, DC Divine Commentary,
DCEzexx M/H/A/T/S   DC Book of Ezekiel Ch xx My/His/Alternate/The/Servants

Title Page GOD Speaks as His Spirit Empowers — I	70. Pursuits of Man — 40
Front Section — II	71. Pursuits of God — 42
GOD Speaks as His Spirit Empowers — III	72. Welfare of Man — 44
	73. Watchtowers of The Saints — 47
Copyright & Publishing — IV	74. Livery of God — 50
Dedication — V	74a Emblem of The Spirit in Use — 53
Acknowledgements — VI	74b Emblem of the Kingdom of God in Use — 54
Prelude — VII	75. Days of Christmas — 55
Content— Order Received — VIII	76. Gratitude of Man — 57
Content— Alphabetical — X	77. Wiles of Woman — 59
Content— Category — XII	78. Allergies of Man — 61
Testimony of	79. Visitation of India — 65
My Book of The Storm — XIV	80. Enquiring of My Spirit — 66
Introduction — XVII	81. Wailing of The Innocent — 68
	82. Righteousness — 70
	83. India is A Land — 73
1. Weather of God — 1	84. Servants in India — 75
2. Wayfarer of God — 3	85. Benevolence of Grace — 77
3. Blessings of The Faithful — 5	86. Tongues of Heaven — 78
4. Fall of Empires — 7	87. Holiness of God — 79
5. Boredom of Man — 9	88. Foundation of My Kingdom — 81
6. Facilities Unknown — 11	89. Days of Leanness — 83
7. Arrows of The Bowman — 12	90. Storming of The Seas — 84
8. Fishing in The Seas — 14	91. Idolatry of Man — 86
9. Lifeline to God — 16	92. Storm of Satan — 88
10. Aggravation of The Soul — 18	93. Storm of Man — 91
11. Settling of The Son — 20	94. Glory of Enthronement — 93
12. Coming Storm — 21	
13. Storm of The Earth — 23	14a. Bk of Ezekiel Intent of DC — 97
62. Variety of Man — 25	14. DCEze01 Vision/s of God, Spirit, wings — 99
63. Storm of God — 27	15. DCEze02 My Prophets, My Spirit, scroll — 108
64. Doves of God — 29	DI Servants (Scribal Note) — 110
65. Absence of God — 31	16. DCEze03 MS Functioning, sacred fare — 111
66. Gift of Tongues — 32	17. DCEze04 MS Prepared, sleep, storm — 114
67. Storm of Fire — 34	18. DI 05 'Overlapping queries' — 116
68. Misery of Man — 37	19. DCEze06 MS Accuracy, deliver, beware — 117
69. Fountain of Youth — 39	20. DCEze07MS Will of God, freewill of man — 119
	21. DCEze08 MS Situational, might, authority — 121

22. DCEze09 MS Consequences, complete, sin 123
23. DCEze10 MS Looks, signs, await, wisdom 126
24. DCEze11 MS Vision transport, will of God 127
25. DI 12 'An End-time example' 128
26. DI 13 'Counsel still valid' 129
27. DCEze14 MS Prophets' caution 130
28. DCEze15 MS become, invitees, adoptees 131
29. DI 16 'Knowledge imparted' 134
30. DI 17 'Oily hands' 135
31. DI 18 'Barabbas' 136
32. DCEze19 MS Situational , err in thinking 137
33. DCEze20 MS Time aware, grace, sin 143
34. DCEze21 MS Sincerity, know, waffles 147
35. DCEze22 MS Wisdom, encounter, idols 151
36. DI 23. 'Vengeance by Jerusalem' 155
37. DCEze24 MS Celebrate, lamb, kid 156
38. DCEze25 MS Called to stand, vengeance 161
39. DI 26 'Sneering at Jerusalem' 167
40. DCEze27 MS Offer, I AM, surprise 168
41. DCEze28 MS Mix, aspects, walk and talk 173
42. DCEze29 MS Change, follow, know 174
43. DCEze30 MS My word, Know those who 176
44. DCEze31 MS Souls, insight, stoop 177
45. DCEze32 MS Serve, God's gifts, answers 181
46. DCEze33 MS I say this day, overcome 185
47. DCEze34 MS Responsibilities, good news 188
48. DI 35 'All with hatred for land of Israel' 190
49. DCEze36 MS Visit, clash, know, see, once 191
50. DCEze37 MS Hear, wisdom, dialogue 197
51. DCEze38 MS Address, process, pray, ram 199
52. DCEze39 MS Familiar, disarm, see, do 202
53. DCEze40 MS Are, offer, value, sort, know 204
54. DCEze41 MS temple, mantle, dead, souls 212
55. DCEze42 HS carry sin, boast, of great evil 220
56. DCEze43 AS *tempt*, uphold, *voyeurs*, repel 223
57. DCEze44 MS dwell, see, know, are, value 225
58. DCEze45 MS can stall, My grace, rebuked 233
59. DCEze46 MS New covenant with Christ 237
60. DCEze47 MS bring, sit, tell, sing, clap 239
61. DCEze48 MS validate, need not, should 242

Appendix— 245
    Journaling and Notes (1) 246
    Journaling and Notes (2) 247
    Journaling and Notes (3) 248
    About the Scribe 249

Book One (3) Reviews
    1st Reviewer: GB 250
    2nd Reviewer: AJE 250
    3rd Reviewer: DN 250

Book Four (3) Reviews
    1st Reviewer: RM 252
    2nd Reviewer: AG 253
    3rd Reviewer: SGS 253

Contents— Alphabetical

DI Divine Intent, DC Divine Commentary,
DCEzexx M/H/A/T/S   DC Book of Ezekiel Ch xx My/His/Alternate/The/Servants

Title Page GOD Speaks as His Spirit Empowers I	17. DCEze04 MS Prepared, sleep, storm 114
Front Section II	18. DI 05 'Overlapping queries' 116
GOD Speaks as His Spirit Empowers III	19. DCEze06 MS Accuracy, deliver, beware 117
Copyright & Publishing IV	20. DCEze07 MS Will of God, freewill of man 119
Dedication V	21. DCEze08 MS Situational, might, authority 121
Acknowledgements VI	22. DCEze09 MS Consequences, complete, sin 123
Prelude VII	23. DCEze10 MS Looks, signs, await, wisdom 126
Content— Order Received VIII	24. DCEze11 MS Vision transport, will of God 127
Content— Alphabetical X	25. DI 12 'An End-time example' 128
Content— Category XII	26. DI 13 'Counsel still valid' 129
Testimony of	27. DCEze14 MS Prophets' caution 130
My Book of The Storm XIV	28. DCEze15 MS become, invitees, adoptees 131
Introduction XVII	29. DI 16 'Knowledge imparted' 134
	30. DI 17 'Oily hands' 135
A	31. DI 18 'Barabbas' 136
Appendix 245	32. DCEze19 MS Situational, err in thinking 137
65. Absence of God 31	33. DCEze20 MS Time aware, grace, sin 143
10. Aggravation of The Soul 18	34. DCEze21 MS Sincerity, know, waffles 147
78. Allergies of Man 61	35. DCEze22 MS Wisdom, encounter, idols 151
7. Arrows of The Bowman 12	36. DI 23. 'Vengeance by Jerusalem' 155
B	37. DCEze24 MS Celebrate, lamb, kid 156
85. Benevolence of Grace 77	38. DCEze25 MS Called to stand, vengeance 161
3. Blessings of The Faithful 5	39. DI 26 'Sneering at Jerusalem' 167
5. Boredom of Man 9	40. DCEze27 MS Offer, I AM, surprise 168
C	41. DCEze28 MS Mix, aspects, walk and talk 173
12. Coming Storm 21	42. DCEze29 MS Change, follow, know 174
D	43. DCEze30 MS My word, Know those who 176
75. Days of Christmas 55	44. DCEze31 MS Souls, insight, stoop 177
89. Days of Leanness 83	45. DCEze32 MS Serve, God's gifts, answers 181
14a. Bk of Ezekiel Intent of DC 97	46. DCEze33 MS I say this day, overcome 185
14. DCEze01 Vision/s of God, Spirit, wings 99	47. DCEze34 MS Responsibilities, good news 188
15. DCEze02 My Prophets, My Spirit, scroll 108	48. DI 35 'All with hatred for land of Israel' 190
DI Servants (Scribal Note) 110	49. DCEze36 MS Visit, clash, know, see, once 191
16. DCEze03 MS Functioning, sacred fare 111	50. DCEze37 MS Hear, wisdom, dialogue 197
	51. DCEze38 MS Address, process, pray, ram 199
	52. DCEze39 MS Familiar, disarm, see, do 202
	53. DCEze40 MS Are, offer, value, sort, know 204

54. DCEze41 MS temple, mantle, dead, souls	212	
55. DCEze42 HS carry sin, boast, of great evil	220	
56. DCEze43 AS *tempt*, uphold, *voyeurs*, repel	223	
57. DCEze44 MS dwell, see, know, are, value	225	
58. DCEze45 MS can stall, My grace, rebuked	233	
59. DCEze46 MS New covenant with Christ	237	
60. DCEze47 MS bring, sit, tell, sing, clap	239	
61. DCEze48 MS validate, need not, should	242	
64. Doves of God	29	

E

74b Emblem of the Kingdom of God in Use	54
74a Emblem of The Spirit in Use	53
80. Enquiring of My Spirit	66

F

6. Facilities Unknown	11
4. Fall of Empires	7
8. Fishing in The Seas	14
88. Foundation of My Kingdom	81
69. Fountain of Youth	39

G

94. Glory of Enthronement	93
76. Gratitude of Man	57
66. Gift of Tongues	32

H

87. Holiness of God	80

I

91. Idolatry of Man	86
83. India is A Land	73

L

9. Lifeline to God	16
74. Livery of God	50

M

68. Misery of Man	37

P

71. Pursuits of God	42
70. Pursuits of Man	40

R

82. Righteousness	70

S

Servants, D Int (Scribal Note)	110
84. Servants in India	75
11. Settling of The Son	20
67. Storm of Fire	34
63. Storm of God	27
93. Storm of Man	91
92. Storm of Satan	88
13. Storm of The Earth	23
90. Storming of The Seas	84

T

86. Tongues of Heaven	78

V

62. Variety of Man	25
79. Visitation of India	65

W

81. Wailing of The Innocent	68
73. Watchtowers of The Saints	47
2. Wayfarer of God	3
1. Weather of God	1
72. Welfare of Man	44
77. Wiles of Woman	59

Appendix—	245
Journaling and Notes (1)	246
Journaling and Notes (2)	247
Journaling and Notes (3)	248
About the Scribe	249
Book One (3) Reviews	
1st Reviewer: GB	250
2nd Reviewer: AJE	250
3rd Reviewer: DN	250
Book Four (3) Reviews	
1st Reviewer: RM	252
2nd Reviewer: AG	253
3rd Reviewer: SGS	253

Contents— Category

DI Divine Intent, DC Divine Commentary,
DCEzexx M/H/A/T/S   DC Book of Ezekiel Ch xx My/His/Alternate/The/Servants

Title Page GOD Speaks as His Spirit Empowers	I
Front Section	II
GOD Speaks as His Spirit Empowers	III
Copyright & Publishing	IV
Dedication	V
Acknowledgements	VI
Prelude	VII
Content— Order Received	VIII
Content— Alphabetical	X
Content— Category	XII
Testimony of My Book of The Storm	XIV
Introduction	XVII

Div Com on Bk of Ezekiel (48)

14a. Bk of Ezekiel Intent of DC 97
14. DCEze01 Vision/s of God, Spirit, wings 99
15. DCEze02 My Prophets, My Spirit, scroll 108
     DI Servants (Scribal Note) 110
16. DCEze03 MS Functioning, sacred fare 111
17. DCEze04 MS Prepared, sleep, storm 114
18. DI 05 'Overlapping queries' 116
19. DCEze06 MS Accuracy, deliver, beware 117
20. DCEze07MS Will of God, freewill of man 119
21. DCEze08 MS Situational, might, authority 121
22. DCEze09 MS Consequences, complete, sin 123
23. DCEze10 MS Looks, signs, await, wisdom 126
24. DCEze11 MS Vision transport, will of God 127
25. DI 12 'An End-time example' 128
26. DI 13 'Counsel still valid' 129
27. DCEze14 MS Prophets' caution 130
28. DCEze15 MS become, invitees, adoptees 131
29. DI 16 'Knowledge imparted' 134
30. DI 17 'Oily hands' 135
31. DI 18 'Barabbas' 136
32. DCEze19 MS Situational, err in thinking 137
33. DCEze20 MS Time aware, grace, sin 143
34. DCEze21 MS Sincerity, know, waffles 147
35. DCEze22 MS Wisdom, encounter, idols 151
36. DI 23. 'Vengeance by Jerusalem' 155
37. DCEze24 MS Celebrate, lamb, kid 156
38. DCEze25 MS Called to stand, vengeance 161
39. DI 26 'Sneering at Jerusalem' 167
40. DCEze27 MS Offer, I AM, surprise 168
41. DCEze28 MS Mix, aspects, walk and talk 173
42. DCEze29 MS Change, follow, know 174
43. DCEze30 MS My word, Know those who 176
44. DCEze31 MS Souls, insight, stoop 177
45. DCEze32 MS Serve, God's gifts, answers 181
46. DCEze33 MS I say this day, overcome 185
47. DCEze34 MS Responsibilities, good news 188
48. DI 35 'All with hatred for land of Israel' 190
49. DCEze36 MS Visit, clash, know, see, once 191
50. DCEze37 MS Hear, wisdom, dialogue 197
51. DCEze38 MS Address, process, pray, ram 199
52. DCEze39 MS Familiar, disarm, see, do 202
53. DCEze40 MS Are, offer, value, sort, know 204
54. DCEze41 MS temple, mantle, dead, souls 212
55. DCEze42 HS carry sin, boast, of great evil 220
56. DCEze43 AS *tempt*, uphold, *voyeurs*, repel 223
57. DCEze44 MS dwell, see, know, are, value 225
58. DCEze45 MS can stall, My grace, rebuked 233
59. DCEze46 MS New covenant with Christ 237
60. DCEze47 MS bring, sit, tell, sing, clap 239
61. DCEze48 MS validate, need not, should 242

Good News (4)

64. Doves of God 29
69. Fountain of Youth 39
71. Pursuits of God 42
75. Days of Christmas 55

My Banner (1)

74. Livery of God	50
74a Emblem of The Spirit in Use	53
74b Emblem of the Kingdom of God in Use	54

My Grace (5)

3. Blessings of The Faithful	5
68. Misery of Man	37
80. Enquiring of My Spirit	66
83. India is A Land	73
85. Benevolence of Grace	77

My Love (3)

62. Variety of Man	25
65. Absence of God	31
67. Storm of Fire	34

My Return (1)

11. Settling of The Son	20

Preparation (28)

1. Weather of God	1
2. Wayfarer of God	3
4. Fall of Empires	7
5. Boredom of Man	9
6. Facilities Unknown	11
7. Arrows of The Bowman	12
8. Fishing in The Seas	14
9. Lifeline to God	16
10. Aggravation of The Soul	18
12. Coming Storm	21
13. Storm of The Earth	23
66. Gift of Tongues	32
70. Pursuits of Man	40
72. Welfare of Man	44
77. Wiles of Woman	59
78. Allergies of Man	61
79. Visitation of India	65
81. Wailing of The Innocent	68
82. Righteousness	68
84. Servants in India	75
86. Tongues of Heaven	78
87. Holiness of God	80
88. Found'n of My Kingdom	81
89. Days of Leanness	83
90. Storming of The Seas	84
91. Idolatry of Man	86
92. Storm of Satan	88
93. Storm of Man	91
94. Glory of Enthronement	93

The Cross (2)

73. Watchtowers of The Saints	47
76. Gratitude of Man	57

The End-time (1)

63. Storm of God	27

Appendix—	245
Journaling and Notes (1)	246
Journaling and Notes (2)	247
Journaling and Notes (3)	248
About the Scribe	249

Book One (3) Reviews

1st Reviewer: GB	250
2nd Reviewer: AJE	250
3rd Reviewer: DN	250

Book Four (3) Reviews

1st Reviewer: RM	252
2nd Reviewer: AG	253
3rd Reviewer: SGS	253

Testimony of My Book of The Storm

"This day,
    I speak to the nations of The Earth,
        the peoples of The Earth,
        the tongues of The Earth
      so they may be aware of what is on the way,
      so they may be prepared for what is round the corner,
      so they may have the foresight to see what is just below the horizon of man.

    I speak to encourage preparation for the tempests of the days,
            the floodings of the days,
            the shakings of the days,
            the deserts of the days,
            the hunger of the days,
            the butchery of the days.

    I speak to man of the days of his coming storm:
        of his desolation;
        of his tribulation;
        of his mourning;
        of his fleeing;
        of his starving;
        of his isolation.

    I speak to man of the days of his coming storm wherein he will be in need
                of sanctuary.

    I speak to My people that they may not be left to wander,
        that they may not be left unsheltered,
        that they may not be left to hunger,
        that they may not be left bereft of the necessities of life.

    I speak to My people that they may read in wisdom of the quartering of The Earth,
        of the storm of pestilence which follows on the heels
                of mourning,
        of the storm of fire which precedes the storm of butchery—
    where freewill runs rampant until exhaustion seals a day.

    For the season which holds the days of thunder approaches as a whirlwind
                in the clouds.

    For the season of consternation to man is like he has never seen before,
            the like of which he will not see again.

    For the season which approaches has been long foretold by God,
        has been made aware to man,

has been making man complacent because of
non-appearance,
has been building to a climax which will test
man to his core.

For the season of fullness of arrival will display man at his best,
will display man at his worst,
will display the upholding of the word
in waiting.

For the time of forbearance will adjust:
the attitude of man;
the outlook of man;
the surroundings of man;
the presence of man;
the beliefs of man,
The Faith of man.

For the onset of the season of tribulation will test the survival of man who is
found with Faith missing from his heart.

For the season soon to be evident before the eyes of man will not wait out the
procrastination of man.

For the season of tribulation terminates in closure of the gate of Grace,
is about to test the preparation of man to meet
his God,
is about to affirm judgment before the great
white throne,
is about to vindicate His word:
where man finally acknowledges he dwells within
the end-times planned by God.

I,
   The Lord Jesus,
      say to man this day,
         'Foolish is he who fails the test of urgency,
            who continues in denial,
            who lingers on the fence,
            who sits there still—
               even as it falls.'

I,
   The Lord Jesus,
      say to man this day,
         'My hand in recognition is offered,
            is extended,
            is firm within its grasp:
         to uplift those bogged and stranded;

to greet those who do call out;
to usher in all who knock—
thereby to cause the door to open in a welcome borne for man.' "

Appreciatively received from The Lord for use in this, His book.

My Content Study Aid

Introduction

These Divine texts mostly consist of Truth Statements intermixed with counselling and are presented for serious contemplation as to their ramifications and how we approach them in the conclusions we may draw. For they are filled with great significance for these present times.

I testify here to one and all that these texts are not of my writing nor instigation. These texts do not stand alone but smoothly build on the preceding ones as if designed as an unfolding story with an establishing foundation. On the original individual documents the scribe has begun each Divine call with the words: 'And I hear The Lord Jesus saying,' "…". It does not appear necessary to have this phrase repetitively introducing each call in this book. Please take it, therefore, as a 'given' as to the stated origin both by testimony and by claim.

The style of the book preserves the scribal comments in italics; while double quotation marks " " denote and enclose text of a Divine origin. British spelling is used for reasons of national culture. Layout simplifies ease of reading and personal study. Each call itself may be accurately searched from within His website. A concordance or a thesaurus has not been used at any stage prior to, during, or after the receiving of these texts. A dictionary (Oxford Concise™) has sometimes been used to comprehend fully, the words of the Divine voice used in expressing His intent. Because the texts have been received via dictation spoken by the Divine voice directly into the mind, the punctuation is subject to human interpretation. Occasionally however, when required for clarity or emphasis, the capitalisation of words, together with the paragraphing, have also been indicated by the Divine. Minor spelling 'typos' are scribal and the punctuation, together with the titles, usually are, but not always. Multiple subject matters sometimes occur in a particular call which precludes the call's naming being entirely appropriate with respect to descriptive accuracy.

Attached to the end of most items is 'My Content Study Aid' inserted at the request of The Lord Jesus to enhance the benefits found in meditating on and understanding the 'Hows' and 'Whys' of the truth statements and His counselling as found herein. If no such Study Aid exists at the end of an item then there are additional Journaling & Notes pages provided in the Appendix. Please remember this is your book to use in the way which best serves your growth within the discipleship of God.

Great care has been taken to ensure scribal accuracy in hearing and transcribing what are now these printed pages of Divinely originated texts. Every word is as received without later omissions, additions, substitutions or edits. May The Holy Spirit so testify as such to every enquiring soul.

The Scribe,
Hamilton,
New Zealand

The Weather of God

"The weather of man is not that forecast by God,
        is not that as assembled by God,
        is not that as prepared by God in the present for man to experience
                              in his future.

The weather of man is concentrated on the here and now,
        reports on the vagaries,
        seeks determinants among the components known to God.

The weather of man could be called a mixture of composites,
        a brewing within a distillery,
        a seething at the shore line where the rocks do churn,
        a settling of the clouds which never carry rain,
        a flooding of the rivers which the dams cannot forestall,
        a trembling of The Earth when his juggernauts traverse.

The weather of man does not discern,
        does not attribute,
        does not foresee,
        does not allocate to cause—
        the majesty,
        the grandeur,
        the authority of all which God holds within His hand,
                of all which God impels by declaration,
                of all which was and is and shall be within the oversight
                                          of God.

Beware the weather of God when He twirls a cloud.
Beware the weather of God when He settles the strains within The Earth.
Beware the weather of God when He changes a sheet upon a bed.
Beware the weather of God when He awakens a mount from slumber.

    For then the plume does rise to mark a release point of The Earth.
    For then a wave uplifts to wash the shorelines of The Earth.
    For then the ripples spread to even out the force paths of contraction.

    For then the power of God displays in might,
                      in majesty,
                      in awe,
                      before the senses of man—
        as the air in motion far surpasses the conceptual gradients of man.

    So then man should discern the origin,
        should discern the onset,

should discern the pattern.

So then man should search the book,
> long since written,
>> which indicates a season within an age,
>> which indicates a change of pace,
>> which indicates a second coming.

So then man should note that which speaks of the birth pangs of great relevance,
> of the birth pangs of the troubling,
> of the birth pangs of the tribulation
>> of man.

So it is as long since foretold.
So it is as the pages turn.
So it is as the time draws near.
So it is as Grace prepares to depart.
So it is as the prophets speak.
So it is as God lifts the key which enables access.
So it is as the curtain rises will man soon experience all which lies beyond the veil."

My Content Study Aid

The Wayfarer of God

"The wayfarer of God has a special relationship with God,
                has a special empathy with God,
                has a special time with God.

The wayfarer on the highway,
 the wayfarer on the byway—
                both can know a walk with God,
                both can know the quietness of the footfall,
                both can know The Holiness of silence.

The wayfarer known to God does not stumble over the stepping stones of God,
                does not impede the tasking of God,
                does not have shoes upon his feet which squelch in the
                                          company of God.

The wayfarer seeking God reads the signposts on the way,
                tastes the fare encountered,
                notes the turning points of life.

The wayfarer finding God testifies in the encounters,
                sings in the presence of the tongues,
                praises in the dawn,
                worships in the dusk,
                prays in seeking wisdom,
                rejoices in the counsel.

The wayfarer rebuked by God grows actively in righteousness,
                grows conspicuously in wisdom,
                grows skilfully in knowledge,
                grows spiritually in Faith,
                grows repentantly in application,
                grows humbly in experience,
                grows attentively in listening.

The wayfarer settling-in with God exhibits a change of heart,
                has no dust upon his shoes,
                has fingers where once were claws,
                has lips which no longer pass profanities,
                has a tongue from which blasphemy is banished.

The wayfarer delighting in God has discipleship to the fore,
                has evangelism in his heart,
                has righteousness dominant in his spirit,
                has agapé love embedded in his soul,

has attentiveness to the being of his brother—
with no averted eyes.

The wayfarer sought by God may need to slow his pace,
may need to unplug his ears,
may need to be attentive to the still small voice of Faith.

The wayfarer sought by God may need to review a dream,
may need to discover the whereabouts of the living water,
may need to avail himself of Grace.

The wayfarer sought by God may have a destiny in question,
may have a history of neglect,
may have uttered a call for help.

The wayfarer sought by God should not decline assistance,
should not postpone the decision of today,
should not ascribe probity to evolution—
as it stagnates as a misshapen lopsided theory of man.

The wayfarer sought by God should rejoice in his creation,
should rejoice in his intended future,
should rejoice at The Grace on offer to him through the
sacrifice of God.

The wayfarer sought by God should rejoice at the integrity of the martyrs who witnessed
to the truth,
should rejoice at the proximity of the end-times plan
of God,
should rejoice at the evidence provided by
the loving God—
all of which is laid before him,
as it surrounds him,
as it interacts with him—
for the building of his Faith."

My Content Study Aid

_____
_____
_____
_____
_____
_____

The Blessings of The Faithful

"The blessings of the faithful are the fruits of God,
        are from the laden boughs of The Lord,
        are the pearls from the reigning of The Holy Spirit.

The blessings of the faithful fall from the triumvirate of God,
        the trinity of God,
        the threefold Godhead—
            long worshipped in unity of being by man.

The blessings of the faithful vary with the time of man,
        vary with the season of man,
        vary with the age of man.

The blessings of the faithful are receipted for the future,
        are receipted for the present,
        are receipted as accruals from the past.

The blessings of the faithful sometimes remain unnoticed,
        sometimes are shared around,
        sometimes are trodden underfoot.

The blessings of the faithful are in response to prayer,
        are in response to righteousness,
        are in response to a change of heart.

The blessings of the faithful denote the favour of The Lord,
        denote membership of the household of God,
        denote a child of God within the covenant of Grace,
        denote the active fear of God,
        denote the footfalls on the staircase of discipleship.

The blessings of the faithful are in the absence of the curses,
        are in the absence of demonic influence,
        are in the absence of the lies of record.

The blessings of the faithful are in the absence of a spirit which is but warm,
        are in the absence of a spirit which has no desire to grow as
            it lingers on the milk,
        are in the absence of a spirit with a resentful roaming soul.

The blessings of the faithful cover all aspects of the life of man,
        all wherein there is an interaction with his God of love:
            his birth,
            his years of immaturity,
            his marriage with its fruit,
            his years of maturity,

his grandchildren of delight,
his time of testimony—
of the experience of a life in preparation.

The blessings of the faithful reflect the closeness to the auspices of God,
reflect the accompanied walk with God,
reflect the brightness of The Light within a life.

The blessings of the faithful speak of the manifest benevolence of God:
the manifest love of The Father,
the manifest sacrifice of The Son,
the manifest giftings of The Spirit.

The blessings of the faithful speak of the intensity of the blessings,
the outpourings of the tongues,
the guidance of The Holy Spirit,
the loving oversight of God.

The blessings of the faithful include the rebukes of God,
include the rights to act,
include the calls to tasks of allocation,
include the strengthening of trust,
include the approval of God in His ambassadors at large.

The blessings of the faithful carry:
the witnessing of signs;
the marvelling at wonders;
the participation in the miracles of declaration;
the gratitude of,
the benefit to,
the honouring of,
the intent of,
the speech of,
the answering of,
His servants and the recipients of His Grace:
as all is fulfilled within His will—
by the blood of The Lamb and the power of testimonies:
in action through Faith in The Name above all names."

My Content Study Aid

_____
_____
_____
_____

The Fall of Empires

"The fall of empires is rarely the work of God,
        is rarely The Will of God,
        is rarely at the behest of God.

The fall of empires often lies within the machinations of man,
                of all which has gone before,
                of wayward behaviour typed
                      as normal,
                of dealings in the darkness,
                of decay met by indifference,
                of extensions in authority which
                      ignored the cost.

The fall of empires facilitates the growth of nations,
        facilitates the diversity of cultures,
        facilitates the welcoming of freedom.

The fall of empires terminates the tyrant,
        terminates the imposition of the law,
        terminates the speaking in a foreign tongue,
        terminates the demands for taxes,
        terminates the armies of might,
        terminates the terror of the night.

The fall of empires brings joy to the governed,
        brings sadness at demise,
        brings potential to experiment,
        brings exuberance at the content of the morrow.

The fall of empires sees a page that turns on history,
        sees the passing of command,
        sees the farewelling of extravagance,
        sees the raising of a generation within the bounds of promise.

The fall of empires sees the dismissing of the guard,
        sees the doors unlocked,
        sees the files come to the fore,
        sees the absence of the curfew,
        sees the dancing in the streets,
        sees the army in its barracks.

The fall of empires speaks of a new beginning,
        transfers the seat of power,
        inaugurates the dissident,
        straightens all the armchairs,

>   secures the empty palace,
>   restructures the citadels of injustice,
>   targets harmony and peace.
>
> The fall of empires can be of short duration,
>   can be extensively drawn out,
>   can be split in fragmentation,
>   can be dealt with as a whole.
>
> The fall of empires can be met with bloodshed,
>   can be when life is put in peril,
>   can be through the sword of man,
>   can be in the presence of The Spirit—
>   without the loss of life."

My Content Study Aid

The Boredom of Man

"The vacationing of man spreads across the seasons of his life.

The vacationing of man,
 the holidaying of man,
  relieves the boredom of the scenes in which he dwells,
                in which he lives,
                in which he plays,
                in which he works,
                in which he seeks a change of pace,
  the boredom which he perceives in his surrounds as failure to excite.

The environment of God should not be included as a breeding ground of boredom
                                        to man—
                in which he praises,
                in which he fears,
                in which he worships the being of his God.

The environment of God is expressive and constructive,
        is attainable and rewarding,
        is experiential and developing.

The environment of God is a wonder in which to be,
        a wonder to see the progress,
        a wonder to be occupied in tasks,
        a wonder to minister under guidance,
        a wonder to share a testimony,
        a wonder to hear the bidden word of God.

The boredom of man is the residue of dissatisfaction,
        is the residue of disappointment,
        is the residue of repetition.

The boredom of man stems from the discouragement of despair,
        stems from the sting of atheism as it kills all hope,
        stems from the repetition of addiction,
        stems from awakening from a stupor,
        stems from the misery of neglect of a sleepy soul which does not
                                know salvation,
        stems from the agnostic who no longer seeks his God.

The boredom of man is a veil of compromise which obscures the target,
        is a veil of smoke laid before the eyes,
        is a veil behind which all is designated as not worth the effort
                                of discovery.

The boredom of man strikes the slothful in their inactivity,
> impinges on the incapacitated with an idle mind,
> confirms the status quo to those who do not seek,
>> those who are caught up in a circle of containment,
>> those who look to others for their source of inspiration,
>> those who do not venture beyond familiarity.

The vacationing of man is an interruption born of desperation,
>> born of the desire for a time of relaxation,
>> born of the quest for something new,
>> born of the seeking of a break from drudgery.

The vacationing of man can be planned into obscurity,
> can be rather hit and miss.

The vacationing of man is felt within the pocket,
> is felt within the memory,
> is felt within the dawning of discoveries,
> is felt within an attitude of certainty in the spirit,
> is felt within the soul as it clambers to be free,
> is felt within the body as it welcomes the return of vigour.

The boredom of man can be despatched from within a mindset,
> can be circumscribed for conquering,
> can be discharged as a victory by the overcomer,
> can be removed by prayer."

My Content Study Aid

Facilities Unknown

"The bed of man is a rarity on The Earth,
        is mostly a construct of unfamiliarity,
        is in use only by the few.

The bed of man speaks of allocation of a room,
        of comfort piled on comfort,
        of facilities unknown so therefore absent from the dreams.

Facilities unknown can not be the source of envy,
        can not give rise to jealousy,
        can not imagine water from a tap,
        can not select the choice of heat.

Facilities unknown are open to discovery,
        may be seen as images from afar,
        may be carried by the voice upon return,
        may be the subject of reports as a source of wonder,
        may be the seat of miracles when there is little understanding,
        may be made into a god with its form of worship.

Facilities unknown may venture into territories of inspection,
        may announce the presence of their being,
        may encourage acquisition by adaption,
        may be sought as desirable in the eyes of the beholder,
        may bring about a change in the environment,
        may populate a vacuum of experience.

Facilities unknown within an enclave speaks of a barrier between an enclave
                                                                                with existence,
                speaks of an isolation,
                speaks of a rejection,
                speaks of a separation,
                speaks of a mystery of advantage,
                speaks of a lack of knowledge.

Facilities unknown on Earth may be known in Heaven.
Facilities unknown in the kingdom of darkness may be known in The Kingdom of light.
Facilities unknown in mortality may be known in eternity.

  So what is rare upon The Earth may be common in Heaven.
  So what is undreamt of on The Earth may populate the heavens.
  So what is practical on The Earth may be impractical in Heaven.

  For as facilities unknown question knowledge unrevealed,
    so the discovering of facilities confirm the surfacing of knowledge."

The Arrows of The Bowman

"The bow of The Lord has arrows which can speak,
        has arrows which can testify,
            has arrows fitted with the warhead of the tongue.

The bow of The Lord has arrows not loosed to maim,
        has arrows not loosed to kill,
            has arrows not loosed to bring the target down.

The bow of The Lord has a quiver which is empty,
        a quiver which awaits selection,
            a quiver which awaits for an arrow proved to be true in flight.

The quiver of the bow accepts arrows of any length,
        accepts arrows of any girth,
        accepts arrows of any colour.

The quiver of the bow holds an arrow without complaint,
        holds an arrow until it is needed,
        holds an arrow until it is plucked and shot.

The quiver of the bow encircles and constrains,
        guards the arrows deemed as true,
        dresses each arrow with a blessing prior to its release.

Each arrow of the bow is a missive with a message,
        is without a barb that buries in the flesh,
        is as a two-edged sword in its effect.

Each arrow of the bow follows in the wake of the rider on the white horse,
        follows in the wake of the call to service,
        follows in the wake of the mounting of a steed,
        follows in the wake of righteousness personified,
        follows in the wake of the oversight of God.

Each arrow of the bow is released upon command,
        is set to attend at a divine appointment,
        is prepared to carry and to follow the tasking of the day.

Each arrow of the bow is empowered by supreme authority,
        is equipped with gifts as needed,
        is established as an envoy on a mission,
        is pointed in a direction aimed at a known address,
        is always under guidance to the target,
        is enabled to transmit the results of flight.

Each arrow of the bow is recovered,

> is mended for a dent,
> is accepted for a further flight as a willing volunteer.
>
> Each arrow of the bow sings a song of joy as it travels on its journey,
> shouts with exuberance as it meets its target,
> sings a song of victory as it is reclaimed to remount upon a steed.
>
> Each arrow of the bow experiences the confidence of the bowman,
> experiences the honouring of the message entrusted for delivery,
> experiences the effect of change
> as the message did proclaim,
> as the word foretold,
> as the arrow delivered with boldness and
> with Faith."

My Content Study Aid

The Fishing in The Seas

"The fishing in the seas is a cause of acrimony between the nations,
        those with rights declared by man,
        those with imagined rights when a signature is not appended.

The fishing in the seas sees a conflict in rationing by nations,
        sees an area preserved by one invaded by another,
        sees mother ships with children wrestle with the seas,
        sees empty boats with sails lying idle on the seas,
        sees the flags of nations which garner—
            leaving with the day—
            encroaching with the night—
        bringing knowledge without wisdom to their activities at sea.

The fishing in the seas is the rattle of the winches,
        is the netting of the trawl,
        is the netting of the drift.

The fishing in the seas requires a craft of means with the sensors of today,
            with teamwork to the fore,
            with markets willing to accept.

The fishing in the seas is a search for the bounty of the catch,
        is a search for the highly valued,
        is a search for the filling of the holds.

The fishing in the seas has effort in the hooking of a shoal;
        in the processing of the meat;
        in making science the scape-goat—
        in the take of false pretences.

    For as the fishing in the seas is part of the dominion of man,
        is part of the meal of man,
        is part of the recreation of man,
        is part of the livelihood of man:
   so man should apply wisdom to his management,
        apply wisdom to his appetite,
        apply wisdom to the sustainability of the cropping of the sea.

  So the fishing in the seas should carry the wisdom to maintain what is already there,
        should carry the integrity of the quota which instils
                no waste,
      should carry the welfare of the birds,
        the welfare of the animals:
            as they interlock both on and in the seas.

For the fishing in the seas is dependent on the health of the seas:
>> is dependent on the temperature of the seas,
>> is dependent on the cycling of the seas,
>> is dependent on the content of the ether of The Earth—
>>>> which forms the breath of man.

For as the seas no longer transport so man encounters lack.
For as the seas fail to nourish so man knows deprivation.
For as the seas energize so man suffers great distress.

For as the seas reclaim so man discovers his tenure of the land:
>> when the seas remove the footprints from the shorelines of The Earth."

My Content Study Aid

The Lifeline to God

"Numerous are the servants of The Lord,
 numerous are the requests of The Lord,
 numerous are the replies of The Lord,
 numerous are the relationships of The Lord,
 numerous are the invitations of The Lord,
 numerous are the acceptances of The Lord.

Numerous are the interactions of The Lord with man.

For The Lord has adopted the being of man,
 has singled out each individually,
 cares for one as much for all,
 counsels each by His Spirit as the need arises,
 rebukes each when a future life is threatened,
 has set signposts for each life where turning points arise.

For The Lord would see all arriving safely home,
 would see the enjoyment of the progress in a journey of freewill,
 would see the growth in Faith that was not forestalled,
 would see the power of testimonies fall upon the head of man,
 would see the rejoicing of the angels as the garlands are bestowed,
 would see the celebrations as each child of God returns,
 would see the acclamations of The Saints who are at the welcome.

For The Lord has paved the way with a walk of wonder,
 has paved the way with a light before the feet,
 has paved the way with reconciliation,
 has paved the way with the soul's redemption,
 has paved the way with the bearing of the sins of man,
 has paved the way with an offering of Grace,
 has paved the way for the inheritance of man.

The inheritance of man arises with The Son,
 arises from The Father,
 arises in the confirmation of The Holy Spirit.

The inheritance of man is as written in the word,
 is as originating from The Cross,
 is as empowered by the empty grave.

The inheritance of man is as promised within God's new covenant with man.

The new covenant with man is one of reconciliation as it mends a broken relationship,
 is one of replacing law with Grace,
 is one of finding an acceptable sacrifice for sin,

is one of Faith with commitment as the basis of
directed belief,
is one of repentance with acknowledgement of the sins of
the past,
is one of water baptism which cleanses the soul.

The new covenant with man is one of baptism of The Spirit which frees the senses of
man for the lifeline to a new beginning.

The lifeline to a new beginning expands the capabilities of man,
enables the tongue to speak,
enables the spirit to interpret,
activates the ears to hear,
sensitizes the skin to touch,
brings a vision to the eyes,
allows access to the scent,
confirms the giftings present,
bestows the gifts implicit in requests.

The lifeline to God is capable of two-way communication."

My Content Study Aid

_____
_____
_____
_____
_____
_____
_____
_____
_____
_____
_____
_____
_____
_____
_____
_____
_____
_____
_____

The Aggravation of The Soul

"The aggravation of the soul is an area of concern to God;
                should be an area of concern to man.

The aggravation of the soul shrieks a note of warning to the spirit.

The aggravation of the soul is a subject of reports outside the mind of man.

The aggravation of the soul speaks of sensitivities not dealt with,
                of depths which are yet to see The Light,
                of plumb-lines of potential righteousness which still
                              tend to bend and sway.

The aggravation of the soul requires a concerted effort
                by he who would have his spirit in control,
                by he who may insist on silence by his lips while annoyance
                              casts temptation for an outburst,
                by he who would be an overcomer both in spirit and in deed.

The aggravation of the soul may have many triggers of irritation,
                may have defensive signs of insult,
                may have conflicts bred of culture,
                may have the taking of offence with recurring recall,
                may have a failure to erase when forgiveness is to the fore,
                may have misinterpretation which floods and inundates in the
                              absence of understanding,
                may have a lack of common sense which circles wisdom
                              as essential.

The aggravation of the soul can destroy a walk with God,
                can hand a victory to the foe of man,
                can bring regret without remorse,
                can place a shadow before The Son.

The aggravation of the soul can concentrate on trivia,
                can ignore the critical.

The aggravation of the soul can supervise the minors,
                can overlook the majors.

The aggravation of the soul can be a starting point of a downhill slide,
                can continue to gather speed,
                can be as a snowball on a slope,
                can be ignorant of the crevasse which would engulf.

The aggravation of the soul can accumulate the muck ready for a mud slide,
                can accumulate emotions until the bursting of the tank,

           can address matters with imagined truth under the guise of
                      false confessions,
           can save and certify as true that which has blame attached
                      to others.

The aggravation of the soul is a serious condition in the sight of God,
        is a serious condition in the sight of the perceptive.

The aggravation of the soul should be serious in the sight of those who would overcome,
        should be seriously addressed in order to circumvent the
                capture of the spirit,
        should be the subject of counsel while it is today,
        should be set as due for polishing—
           so it may absorb and reflect without distortion.

The aggravation of the soul is relevant to man in his mortality,
        is in condition to be pruned,
        is to be brought into subjugation to the spirit of man,
        is destined to enhance the ongoing journeying of man,
        is destined to be hugged or rejected by God in the future walk
                      of man."

My Content Study Aid

_____
_____
_____
_____
_____
_____
_____
_____
_____
_____
_____
_____
_____
_____
_____
_____
_____

The Settling of The Son

"The settling of The Son speaks of imminent activity.
The settling of The Son speaks of at home upon a throne.
The settling of The Son speaks of rewards at hand.

The settling of The Son speaks of preparation as if for an Olympic games,
    where the ribbons with the medals have significance of achievement,
        are rewards to those who train,
        are testimonies of ability upon the field of life.

The settling of The Son is of the inheritances due upon His death,
        due upon His rising,
        due upon His coming into His kingdom;
        due unto all adopted as His brothers,
        due unto the martyrs,
        due unto disciples,
        due unto His servants according to
            each call.

The settling of The Son includes the replevin due of Satan.

The settling of The Son commences with the opening of the Book of Life;
    ends with the finality of an audience before the great white throne."

My Content Study Aid

_____
_____
_____
_____
_____
_____
_____
_____
_____
_____
_____
_____
_____
_____

The Coming Storm

"The coming storm encompasses the storm of scripture,
        encompasses the storm of prophecy,
        encompasses the storm of tribulation*,
        encompasses the storm of fire,
        encompasses the storm of Earth,
        encompasses the storm of Satan,
        encompasses the storm of man,
        is about to be upon The Earth,
        is about to tear the fabric of the societies of man,
        is about to be visited upon the distress of man.

For as the storm prevails over the life of man so one has its floodgates opened,
        so one has its surges of discontent,
        so one hearkens to the voice of God,
        so one bows before the waves of The Spirit,
        so one comes in crests and troughs,
        so one peaks in a crescendo,
        so one retreats into the silence of completion.

For as the storm transmits its being into the life of man so man turns
        in understanding,
        so man accesses what he did not know,
        so man suffers unto death for the sin he carries,
        so man bears witness of his heart,
        so man knows a shaking for attention,
        so man surrenders the freewill of his soul,
        so man exhibits his malevolence set free.

So the coming storm is the prelude to the end of Grace,
        is either the prelude to a change of heart,
        or the prelude to reinforcement of what already is,
        is either the prelude to a welcome by the founder of
        the universe,
        or the prelude to segregation via judgment well foretold.

The coming storm tests the preparation,
        tests the knowledge,
        tests The Wisdom,
        tests the spirit,
        tests the soul,
        of the being of creation known as man."

Scribal Note:
* Refer: 'The End-time Experience of Tribulation' Bk 4, 'GOD Speaks to Man in the End-time',

also: 'The Tribulation of Life' Bk 7, 'GOD Speaks to His Edifice'
also: 'The Fire and The Tribulation' Bk 1, 'GOD Speaks of Return and Bannered'.

My Content Study Aid

The Storm of The Earth

"The storm of The Earth has not seen its like before,
        has not seen the destruction wrought,
        has not seen the suffering incurred,
        has not seen the difficulty of repair,
        has not seen the magnitude of claims,
        has not seen the laying waste on such a scale.

The storm of The Earth invades the privacy of man,
        invades the places of possession,
        invades the caverns of retreat,
        invades the secular and the carnal,
        invades the idol spots of Earth.

The storm of The Earth screams at the profane,
        screams at the destroyers of unfolding life,
        screams at the visitors of ill repute,
        screams at the sequences of sin,
        screams at the pitfalls laid for man.

The storm of The Earth has a centre of calm,
        has a centre with an eye,
        has a centre open to the heavens.

The storm of The Earth is selective in its posture,
        is selective in its force applied,
        is selective in its path,
        is selective in its retreat,
        is selective in its avoidance,
        is selective in its tumult.

The storm of The Earth separates and segregates,
        splinters and filters,
        vibrates and shakes,
        carries and removes:
              deposits as a whole;
              scatters as grains of salt as they issue from the salt cellar.

The storm of The Earth has the ability to leap-frog,
        has the ability to hit and miss,
        has the ability to come and to depart,
        has the ability to seek and to destroy,
        has the ability to purge or to cleanse the faces of The Earth,
                the facades of The Earth,
                the facilities of The Earth,

>   the factories of The Earth.
> The storm of The Earth leaves little time for recuperation,
>   leaves little time for shoring up,
>   leaves little time for the emotions of man,
>   leaves little time for the unrighteous to square up to their soul
>   with their spirit's call."

My Content Study Aid

_____
_____
_____
_____
_____
_____
_____
_____
_____
_____
_____
_____
_____
_____
_____
_____
_____
_____
_____
_____
_____
_____
_____
_____
_____
_____
_____
_____

The Variety of Man

"The variety of man seals the inheritance of Babel.
The variety of man confirms the camp fires of adversity.
The variety of man promotes a call for a common language.

The variety of man denies the commonality of assent,
        denies a footbridge to assembly,
        denies the breaking of the boundaries,
        denies a walk of understanding among the strangers,
        denies the ease of a concerted effort,
        denies forbearance in the interests of the nations.

The variety of man brings unity within diversity of all aspects of the life of man,
        within a common culture,
        within a specific culture,
        within a culture installed by fear of divinity,
        within a culture installed by trade,
        within a culture installed by greed,
        within a culture installed by domination.

The variety of man shares the common needs of life which vary in abundance.

The variety of man knows the seeking of the experience of God.
The variety of man knows the conflict between light and darkness.
The variety of man knows the opposites of love and hate.

The variety of man is reflected in the family tree of conquest:
        of overcoming,
        of sustained viability,
        of living within the searching
                for resources.

The variety of man now dominates The Earth,
        now makes it subservient to his will,
        now incurs the displeasure of the selfish.

The variety of man rebels against authority which intrudes,
        against attempts to enter his measured space on Earth,
        against gratuitous advice which serves another's purpose.

The variety of man separates and divides the resources as discovered,
        the resources as may be,
        the resources of possibility;
    imposes barriers of taste and circumstance:
        of dress,
        of tongues,

of transportation,
of dwellings,
of environment,
of livelihood.

The variety of man wars,
        fights,
        terrorizes,
        subdues:
            until exhaustion outweighs the call for victory;
            surrenders to the foe upon exhaustion of intent;
            carries on the fight upon renewal of intent.

The variety of man enmeshed in a fight for survival uses whatever is at hand,
                whatever can be a weapon,
                whatever serves the goal of
                    overcoming the
                    antagonist of the day.

The variety of man releases military might upon the whim of the few,
        cannot reseal the bottle once The Earth is soaked in blood,
        cannot repeal the actions when pride becomes installed to take the
                pride of place.

The variety of man has a history of conflict,
        has a history arising from satanic influence,
        has a history portraying demonic activities
                vested in the soul of man,
                manifested through the soul of man,
                evidenced by the soul of man.

The variety of man continually tends to side with evil in the application of freewill:
            that which so castrates the future being of man.

The variety of man does not suffer confinement at the hands of the loving God,
        does not suffer preferential treatment before the throne of God,
        does not suffer rejection of hearts accepting change,
        does not suffer exclusion from a relationship with God."

My Content Study Aid

_____

_____

_____

_____

The Storm of God

"The storm of the century is the storm of man;
  the storm of the centuries is the storm of God.

The storm of God has been a long time in the coming onto the horizon of man.

The storm of God is that fulfilling that of which has been long spoken:
                that of which is scheduled for The End-time,
                that of which is scheduled as the prelude to rebirth,
                that of which is scheduled for both the expectant and
                                the surprised.

The storm of God humbles the vain and the proud,
        humbles the selfish and the uncaring,
        humbles the greedy and the trespasser.

  Woe to those who trespass within the precincts of God with unclean hands.

The storm of God clarifies man,
        clarifies The Earth,
        clarifies creation.

The storm of God troubles all aspects of the life of man,
        determines a time of meditation,
            a time of switching,
            a time of cursing,
            a time of blasphemy,
            a time of destruction,
            a time of supervision,
            a time of appreciation.

The storm of God impacts on the environment of man.

The storm of God sallies and recedes,
        advances and retreats,
        demolishes and clears.

The storm of God unfolds and intensifies,
        encroaches and invades,
        encircles and releases.

The storm of God leaves trails which can be traced,
        leaves areas of desolation,
        leaves countries fit for kings,
        leaves nations awaiting governance,
        leaves The Earth ready for renewal.

The storm of God brings mourning and grief to the unprepared for the ways of God,

brings loss and despair to the unaware in denial of the ways of God,
brings the testing of the resolute to stand in defiance of the ways
of God.

The storm of God brings The End-time into the reality of man.

The storm of God brings The End-time before The Multitudes who query.
The storm of God brings The End-time before The Multitudes in waiting.
The storm of God brings The End-time before The Multitudes who die.

The storm of God does not raise the dead.

The storm of God lays waste the citadels of sin:
> the mountains of iniquity,
> the icebergs of depravity,
> the highways of pornography,
> the cities of infidelity,
> the vestiges of violence,
> the enclaves affirming idols.

The storm of God lays waste the workplaces of the devil on the agency of man,
> the sandcastles of Satan on the soul of man,
> the impositions of the demons on the health of man.

The storm of God sequesters the committed spirit with the soul within The Family of God.

The storm of God does not violate the warnings of God,
> does not violate the prepared of God,
> does not violate the incumbents of God.

The storm of God threatens all within the judicature of God,
> threatens all outside The Will of God,
> threatens all the enemies of God.

The storm of God threatens all who ignore The Living God,
> threatens all who prefer to worship idols,
> threatens all who sacrifice under law,
> threatens all who profess to oaths of blood,
> threatens all who have heard yet do not heed the word of God.

The storm of God is a mixture of capabilities,
> is a mixture of responses,
> is a mixture of onslaughts of attention,
> is a mixture of the sufferings of God.

The storm of God is the curtain call for the performance of man."

The Doves of God

"The doves of God abound in Heaven,
        abound among the hosts,
        abound in joy and freedom.

The doves of God abound as emissaries of Grace to the lost,
        as emissaries of peace to the troubled,
        as emissaries of virtue to the wanton.

The doves of God are the initial contact point with the spirit of man,
        manifest as second thoughts,
        give an impression of déjà vu.

The doves of God are seconded by My Spirit,
        are assigned in multiples of three,
        are respecters of the freewill of man.

The doves of God are attuned to The Will of God,
        bring simple messages of possibility,
        confirm the nearness of the divinity of God.

The doves of God neither peck nor claw,
        neither flutter nor squawk,
        neither pester nor prolong.

The doves of God glide and whisper with a coo in passing,
        are not repetitive by nature,
        are not signed by My Spirit.

The doves of God circle overhead as they choose their moment,
        enjoy a slight reaction if the pinprick of the message registers with the spirit of man,
        resume their mingling with the hosts when their message has been sent.

The doves of God are the transmitters of the telegrams to man sent to test the spirit and the soul.

The doves of God are as the seed of Faith which first sensitizes the spirit and the soul.

The doves of God are the placers of the seed in the hope that it will sprout.

The doves of God have no volition to converse separately with man.

The doves of God are obedient and reliable,
        are humble and unflustered,
        are discrete yet self-assured.

The doves of God are unobtrusive yet effective,

>   are the selectors of the soil on offer,
>   are the planters of the seed which can yet lie dormant,
>   which can blossom in its fullness,
>   which can yet succumb to weeds.

The doves of God are in the forefront of the works of God.
The doves of God are the scouts of Heaven.
The doves of God are the planters-out of Faith in the being known as man."

My Content Study Aid

The Absence of God

"The concept of man is not an easy one to postulate,
        is not an easy one to simulate,
        is not an easy one to duplicate,
        is not an easy one to emulate.

The concept of man is fraught with difficulties when there is no original
        on which to base design,
        on which to plot and play,
        on which to scribble and erase.

The concept of man is easy to accept when within the sphere of being,
        when within the sphere of man's reality,
        when within the sphere of the physicality of man.

The mind of man has difficulty in grasping the concept of 'not being',
        the concept of non-existence,
        the impossibility of such odds being attained
        in the actuality of existence.

The mind of man resolves,
        by accepting in support,
        the practicality of evolving that which stands before them.

The mind of man takes the existence of man as 'proof' of the reality of evolution:
        the absence of design discharging God of all input to the freewill
        being in existence,
        deducting the morality of God as the lynchpin
        of behaviour.

So man reduces self-control to be measured by his ethics—
        ethics which are always relative to he who can be the announcer of the day,
        are never absolute in value,
        have no integrity of purpose other than for he
        who shouts the loudest,
        who carries the largest stick,
        who imposes his opinion on those
        with no opinion.

So the agency of man is reduced to the synopsis of the fool in equality with the wise,
        is reduced to the impotence of gibberish from every mind
        of man,
        is able to affirm a topsy-turvy world where good and evil no
        longer have existence—
        becoming mixtures of each other from which everyone can drink
        without fear of conviction."

The Gift of Tongues

"The Father oversees the works of God.

The Son manages the works of God.

The Holy Spirit actions the works of God.

The triumvirate of God is the trinity of God,
>> is the unity of God,
>>> is the point of singularity for the worship of the universe as known to man.

The triumvirate of God works in perfect unison in the functioning of the entity of God.

The entity of God was.

The entity of God is.

The entity of God continues.

The entity of God dwells as in infinity,
> in the concept of eternity,
> outside the time of man,
> as the singularity of existence.

The entity of God is the supreme authority within the universe of man,
> within the universes of creation,
> within the universes yet to be.

The entity of God is currently beyond the comprehension of man in his mortality.

There are no words in any language of man capable of conveying
> that which is known to God,
> that which is known within the heavens of God,
> that which awaits the transition of man into an eternal being.

The use of the parables,
> the metaphors,
> the allegories,
> the similes of man are as God using a sledgehammer of composition in the heavens to crack a nut upon The Earth of man.

The realities of the heavens of God are not directly translatable into the written or the spoken words of man.

The limitations of the vocabularies of man impose repetition of the phrases associated with divinity.

The gift of tongues exemplifies the difficulty of conversing with understanding during the mortality of man.

The gift of tongues exemplifies the extended languages of the heavens apparent on the

> tongue of man,
> exemplifies the difficulty to forge man's comprehension,
> exemplifies the difficulty in man receiving an accurate translation of
> the spoken tongue when constructions are
> missing from the vocabulary of the day.
>
> So this can be likened to Eskimos using English to converse on the subjectiveness
> of snow.
>
> The gift of tongues is the highway of expression built for the use of man
> in talking to his God,
> in speaking forth the messaging of God,
> in receiving blessings when achieving
> fluency both in the
> sending and receiving.
>
> The gift of tongues awaits the exploration of man,
> awaits familiarity through frequency of practice,
> awaits freedom to progress the soul of man.
>
> The gift of tongues awaits the fullness of achievement as designed by God for man.
>
> The gift of tongues summits in direct communication:
> which has no means of interruption;
> which is conversant with the heavens;
> which moves man in preparation into the
> realm of the reality of thought."

My Content Study Aid

_____
_____
_____
_____
_____
_____
_____
_____
_____
_____
_____
_____

The Storm of Fire

"The storm of fire invades The Earth.
The storm of fire falls from Heaven.
The storm of fire is preceded by My Spirit.

The storm of fire catches hold of the tongues of man,
        catches hold of the communities of man,
        catches hold of The Church of God.

The storm of fire catches hold of all who love The Lord.

The storm of fire blazes in The Temples,
        blazes in My Church,
        blazes across nations,
        blazes across seas.

The storm of fire is fed by My Spirit,
        is spread by My Spirit,
        is led by My Spirit.

The storm of fire is a beacon of The Lord,
        is an end-time sign of God,
        is the refuge for the lost.

The storm of fire produces visions of the flames upon—
                the head,
                the arms,
                the hands of man.

The storm of fire abounds throughout The Earth,
        abounds in the remotest of the islands of the seas,
        abounds in the congested cities of the nations.

The storm of fire abounds at the behest of God.

The storm of fire signals to the peoples of The Earth,
        signals all is well to The Saints of God,
        signals the onset of The End-time to all who know not God.

The storm of fire comes to stay,
        does not fade and die,
        invigorates with transformation.

The storm of fire brings confirmation to the wise,
        brings trepidation to the uncommitted,
        brings interest from the non-committed.

The storm of fire brings the seekers to their God.

The storm of fire feeds upon increasing knowledge of God,
        upon the testimonies of The Saints,
        upon the statements of the recently set-alight.

The storm of fire encounters and surrounds,
        gathers round a burnt-out candle so it can be relit,
        gathers round the on-lookers so they can feel the heat.

The storm of fire moves as borne by a great and rushing wind,
        leaps in bounds as embers are blown before,
        kindles afresh within the brushwood The End-time fire of God.

The storm of fire overflows from the chalice of My Spirit,
        that which flames as the torch of incandescence,
        that which is the refiner's fire,
        that which skims the dross off the life of man.

The storm of fire impresses on The Earth the seal of God,
        the claim of God,
        the presence of God.

The storm of fire is the firewall of the heavens for the safe-guarding of the soul of man.

The storm of fire is the shield of God which stands before satanic forces:
        those who would attack the souls of The Saints-in-waiting.

The storm of fire is the tongues of Heaven being brought to The Earth,
        being declared upon The Earth,
        being instated on The Earth.

The storm of fire is unaffected by a fire hose,
        is unaffected by waters of immersion,
        is unaffected by disuse.

The storm of fire is a salutation to the loving God,
        is a status report from deep within a soul,
        is the kindling for an infant who likes the warmth of fire.

The storm of fire is the gale which fans My Spirit's flame into the inferno:
        which crosses all divides,
        which does not obey the fire breaks of man,
        which circumvents the wicked,
        which gently touches all who would reach out.

The storm of fire has speed and velocity of delivery,
        has variation in the flame,
        has variation in the colour,
        has variation in the intensity,
        has variation in the height.

The storm of fire opens mouths in amazement,

        opens mouths in prayer,
        opens mouths in praise,
        opens mouths in worship,
        opens mouths in thanksgiving to the God of love.

The storm of fire is not lightly dismissed by the ignorant,
        is not dismissed by the knowing,
        is affirmed by the wise,
        is adopted by the thoughtful.

The storm of fire carries convincing fare in the inferno of the flames,
        offers food for lambs who play upon the fringes of the flames,
        brings cycles in the flames as they arise with additions to the fare.

The storm of fire achieves the ignition of The Lighthouse of the soul,
        the burning of The Light,
        the trimming of the flame.

The storm of fire tests the welfare of the soul,
        the keenness of the spirit,
        the integrity of The Temple.

The storm of fire brings the balm of Gilead to so dress a soul."

My Content Study Aid

_____

_____

_____

_____

_____

_____

_____

_____

_____

_____

_____

_____

_____

_____

The Misery of Man

"The misery of man dwells within his soul as a captive of his foe,
                      as a captive of lost hope,
                      as a captive without Faith.

The misery of man feeds on his self-pity,
            feeds on past failures of his plans,
            feeds on the blame seen as others.

The misery of man pre-empts his mastery of success,
            pre-empts his willingness to strive,
            pre-empts a sojourn in the sun.

The misery of man greets each day as he expects,
            greets each day with a groan,
            greets each day with a tear upon a heart.

The misery of man greets each day with his burden carried forward through the darkness
                                                                             of the night.
The misery of man greets each day with his troubles of the days gone by.
The misery of man greets each day with the anxieties he fears he will encounter.

The misery of man has no expectation of a rescue,
            has no trust in offered help,
            has no input from his spirit.

The misery of man knows a downward spiral.

The misery of man seeks solitude in silence,
            seeks the passing of the day,
            seeks the passing of the night.

The misery of man has no end within his sight.

The misery of man frequents the darkest depths of man,
            frequents the depths from which it is difficult to return,
            frequents the depths where there is but a glimmer of the sunlight.

The misery of man is tugged ever deeper by the foe,
            is tugged ever deeper by the weight,
            is tugged ever deeper by despair.

The misery of man is tugged ever deeper by the isolation of his soul.

The misery of man succumbs to a circle of entrapment,
            succumbs to a loss of will,
            succumbs to being in a fog.

The misery of man is being impaled on the pitchfork of the devil,

    is being tossed to and fro as a sheaf of wheat,
    is being thrashed until there is nothing left to shed.

The misery of man is a nesting place of vermin,
    is a burrow with a snake,
    is a feeding place of vultures.

The misery of man is festooned in the cobwebs of a cave,
    is imprisoned by a palm tree in the desert,
    is selected by the demons as their playground of the day,
      as their party place at night.

The misery of man is not a guest man should invite into his home.

The misery of man is broken by The Cross,
    is spent by The Cross,
    is healed by what happened on The Cross.

The misery of man is brought to be by the fall of man.

The misery of man is shed under the fall of Grace.

The misery of man is no longer under law.

The misery of man is now uplifted by commitment,
    is now removed by acceptance of the offer of abounding Grace,
    is now dissolved as a cloud of shadows in the fullness of the sun.

The misery of man is a relic of a bygone age.

The misery of man serves up the works of Satan within the freewill of man.

The misery of man cannot survive the encounter with The Cross when man calls out for attention under Grace."

My Content Study Aid

_____
_____
_____
_____
_____
_____
_____
_____
_____
_____

The Fountain of Youth

"The fountain of youth is not something which should be mourned,
        is not something for the yearning of the heart,
        is not the answer to a prayer.
The fountain of youth is the catch-cry of maturity which is looking in the past,
        is the figment of imagination never built on fact,
        is the wistful backward glance at a body supposedly in its prime.
The fountain of youth encompasses the whole of the mortality of man—
        the bursting forth with new life implanted,
        the arising forth with My Spirit's presence,
        the uplifting forth with the blessing of The Father:
            ennobled in the gown of life.
The fountain of youth does not decry the concept;
        rather adjusts the period of validity in the unfolding life of man.
The fountain of youth describes man's early blossoming in a wonderland of discovery:
        as he walks the path of intended destiny,
        as he walks the path where his God looks on
            upon the daily scene,
            upon the nightly scene,
            upon the scene not readily confessed.
The fountain of youth does not condone the mistakes of man,
        does not over-ride the consequences,
        does not neutralize the negatives with positives.
The fountain of youth is not a panacea for the troubles of man,
        the desires of man,
        the immaturity of man.
The fountain of youth describes the highpoint in the mortality of man:
        the fountaining of My Spirit when first the water is turned on,
        the quenching of the thirst as the living water puts a seal upon
                a temple,
        the giftings of My Spirit as the attributes are discovered
                for display,
        the onset of a relationship with God—
            which augurs well for the future life of man."

My Content Study Aid

The Pursuits of Man

"The pursuits of man rarely are the pursuits of God.

The pursuits of man have no promise of success,
        have no promise of reward,
        have no promise of satisfaction,
        have no promise of completion,
        have no promise of need fulfilment,
        have no promise of endurance.

The pursuits of man can be fixated on a goal,
        can target an achievement,
        can satisfy a longing,
        can bring to pass a dream,
        can invite companionship,
        can augment a life.

The pursuits of man can be rewarding to his nature,
        can be disappointing to his spirit.

The pursuits of man can experience great evil,
        can experience great good.

The pursuits of man can vary with the tuning of his character,
        can vary with the impact of his parents,
        can vary with the counsel of his god.

The pursuits of man are variable by day,
        are variable by night,
        are variable by endeavour,
        are variable by slothfulness,
        are variable by wealth,
        are variable by imagination.

The pursuits of man are limited by his environment,
        are limited by his successes,
        are limited by his failures.

The pursuits of man are not limited by God.

The pursuits of man are not limiting of his future.

The pursuits of man should not suffer procrastination.

The pursuits of man should attend to the decisions of the day.

The pursuits of man each carries a parachute to safety,
                an escape clause of great dignity,
                a remission process for mistakes.

The pursuits of man are the groundings in abilities,
                are the acknowledgments of effort,
                are the stretching of the possibilities,
                are the increasing of the probabilities,
                are the journeys in the making,
                are the contributors to the record of freewill.

The pursuits of man fulfil man's aspirations,
                bring satisfaction to his soul,
                uplift his spirit to new heights,
                synchronize his body to his will.

The pursuits of man exchange ignorance for knowledge,
                supplant foolishness with wisdom,
                replace aimlessness with goals.

The pursuits of man can have eternal significance on his wellbeing,
                can impose a stature which commands respect,
                can result in status deserving of great honour.

The pursuits of man can leave him in the grip of Satan;
                can exalt him in the heavens within The Family of God."

My Content Study Aid

The Pursuits of God

"The pursuits of God are the pursuits of His servants.

The pursuits of God extend The Edifice of God.
The pursuits of God enable the works of God.
The pursuits of God vie with the devil for the souls of man.

The pursuits of God embellish and direct,
                adorn and beautify all aspects of creation.

The pursuits of God establish and uphold the onward walk with man.

The pursuits of God are not conducive to a timetable,
                are functionings which have no end.

The pursuits of God result in complexity of function,
                result in simplicity of design,
                result in a testimony of God.

The pursuits of God are the origins of the standards for the pursuits of man.

The pursuits of God typify those pursued by man.
The pursuits of God are the archetypes for the pursuits of man.
The pursuits of God offer assistance to the pursuits of man.

The pursuits of God lay a path for the freewill of man:
                that which is attentive to man attaining his destiny selected
                                            in mortality.

The pursuits of God bear on the physical experience of man,
                bear on the spiritual experience of man,
                bear on the eternal with man constantly in mind.

The pursuits of God are such as will achieve His intent.

The pursuits of God are such as may be governed by the mortality of man,
                are such as may be necessitated by the immortality of man,
                are such as may be enthroned for man in the company of his God.

The pursuits of God are not cough mixtures for The Saints upon their journeys,
                for man in his mortality.

The pursuits of God are as a gown of beauty placed ready for the fitting as the new glove
                of man.

The pursuits of God achieve perfection of display,
                achieve perfection of existence,
                achieve perfection of experience.

The pursuits of God serve myriads of purposes,
>> serve myriads of details,
>> serve myriads of applications.

The pursuits of God include the lacework of the networking of God.

The pursuits of God exceed the imaginings of man in his mortality.

The pursuits of God extend the travel capabilities of man after his mortality.

The pursuits of God extend the scope of man into the eternity of God.

The pursuits of God extend the fellowship of man,
>> by his preparation within mortality,
>> for full fellowship with God."

My Content Study Aid

_____
_____
_____
_____
_____
_____
_____
_____
_____
_____
_____
_____
_____
_____
_____
_____
_____
_____
_____
_____
_____
_____
_____
_____
_____

The Welfare of Man

"The welfare of man is the prime consideration of God.

The welfare of man is subject to the freewill of man.

The welfare of man does not over-ride the acquaintances of man,
                the partnerships of man,
                the companions of man.

The welfare of man does not over-ride the imaginings of man,
                the feelings of man,
                the privations of man:
                      those which emanate from the freewill of man.

The welfare of man does not over-ride the influence of his peers,
                the influence of his creditors,
                the influence of those to which he ascribes status
                      as a figurehead.

The welfare of man does not over-ride the murmurings of demons,
                the invitations of deceit,
                the pressures of the market place of man.

The welfare of man does not protect from the consent of the yoking of man,
        does not protect from the seeking of adrenaline,
        does not protect from the process of addiction.

The welfare of man does not protect from the lack of wisdom,
                from the lack of a relationship with God.

The welfare of man cannot be plead as lacking before the courts of Heaven when arising
                from a non-relationship with God.

The welfare of man is governed by the freewill of man,
            the agency of man,
            the determinator of the destiny of man.

The welfare of man sequences in needs and wants across the gamut of the life of man.

The welfare of man over-rides the evil of the foe of man when subjected to a prayer for
                    assistance in combatting the evil intent,
                            the evil incisions,
                            the evil insertions,
                            the evil placements,
                            the evil motivations,
                            the evil luring—
                                of the foe of man.

The welfare of man is not immune to the wiles of the devil when found alone and
                                        unprepared upon the battlefield.

The welfare of man is assigned to the care of angels upon entry into The Lamb's Book
                                          of Life.

The welfare of man encompasses his spirit and his soul,
        encompasses his body in entirety—
                both in function and perception.

The welfare of man is not the begging of necessity falling under the mantle of mercy—
        for there goes the pleading of a spirit and a soul
                in agreement with the body.

The welfare of man is not he who is caught with stolen bread within his mouth—
        for there goes a man who knows not God.

The welfare of man is not he who plunders the purse for penury while working with
                                      his hands—
        for there goes the endeavours of satanic deceit.

The welfare of man is never seen in action when invoked through the lies of man—
        for there goes a candidate for Hell.

Woe to those who are so foolish in their understanding that they are destined to meet
                                      a liar's fate:
                that their soul should be forever consigned to the fires of Hell;
                that their spirit should fall to the second death;
                that their lack of discipline should bring a life of great promise
                              to such a destiny as this.

The welfare of man should be at the forefront of his care,
            at the forefront of his family,
            at the forefront of his thoughts.

The welfare of man should not be allowed to lapse because considered unimportant.

The welfare of man is critical to God,
        is critical to man,
        is critical to the offspring of his loins.

The welfare of man needs guarding with perseverance,
        needs checks which measure progress,
        needs vitality to support endeavour.

The welfare of man should not dwell among the lonely weeds,
        not dwell among the self-isolated from God,
        not dwell within the enclaves of the liars and the thieves.

The welfare of man should not dwell among the broken reeds.

The welfare of man should not be postponed:

because of a surplus of life still seen to be in store,
because of the supposition that the lifeline is secure
and certain,
because of the assumption that a commitment to a
destiny may not be cut short by
the unexpected call of death,
because of the loss of preparation for a welcome which
would obviate the
need for judgment,
because of the devil's tongue which whispers in the lie,
'Grace is forever there.'

The welfare of man is the prime directive of God to the hosts of Heaven.

The welfare of man is the prime directive of His counsel to the spirit and the soul of man.

The welfare of man is the prime directive from The Father to The Son to The Holy Spirit
that man may not be stranded in
that for which the bells are tolled.

The welfare of man should hearken to the warning cries of his spirit that all is far from
well when a commitment is missing
from the record of his soul."

My Content Study Aid

_____
_____
_____
_____
_____
_____
_____
_____
_____
_____
_____
_____
_____
_____
_____

The Watchtowers of The Saints

"The watchtowers of the saints are mobile and can pivot.

The watchtowers of the saints can inspect quite closely,
                can inspect from a distance,
                can inspect what is of interest.

The watchtowers of the saints are constructed for renewal,
                are constructed for a battle,
                are constructed with great care.

The watchtowers of the saints can turn away,
                can turn towards,
                can crank a siren in emergencies,
                can summon assistance with their problems,
                can peruse a plan approved and filed.

The watchtowers of the saints can repel invaders,
                can protect the base,
                can reinforce the foundations so they will stand firm.

The watchtowers of the saints are positioned to stand before the foe of man,
                are positioned to locate the foes of man,
                are positioned to demolish the high places of the foe.

The watchtowers of the saints have sight lines of clarity,
                have loudspeakers which decry the presence of the foe,
                have strength to overcome the attacks of pain.

The watchtowers of the saints are staffed and manned,
                are out in all the weathers,
                are active with each rising of the sun.

The watchtowers of the saints listen keenly to reports,
                compose and despatch the signals of the day,
                act in unison to tumble the ramparts with their keeps.

The watchtowers of the saints are awake to unauthorised intrusions,
                are prepared to repel the boarders,
                are capable of the clearing of the foe.

The watchtowers of the saints have the armour for defiance,
                the armour of support,
                the armour which deflects.

The watchtowers of the saints know the power of God,
                know the support of God,
                know the gifts of God.

The watchtowers of the saints know the word of God,
>> know the promises of God,
>> know the miracles of God.

The watchtowers of the saints have Faith in the God of whom they serve.

The watchtowers of the saints celebrate the victories of their God,
>> the faithfulness of their God,
>> the upholding of their God.

The watchtowers of the saints have records of the testimonies of their God.

The watchtowers of the saints stand before the foe of man,
>> stand against the foe of man,
>> stand on the foe of man.

The watchtowers of the saints sift the rubble of collapse,
>> deal with remnants of deceit,
>> remove the focus from the foe.

The watchtowers of the saints deny the limelight to the enemy of man,
>> deny him the spotlight in the centre of the stage,
>> deny him the curtain call of life.

The watchtowers of the saints relegate the devil to the proximity of God,
>> consign the evil forces to rampage somewhere else,
>> scatter the presence of the demons from where they like
>>>> to squat.

The watchtowers of the saints maintain a threshold for behaviour,
>> maintain a course without need for adjustment,
>> maintain a boundary of forgiveness,
>> maintain the simplicity of truth,
>> maintain the importance of Faith,
>> maintain the target of a sacrifice,
>> maintain the belief in grace.

The watchtowers of the saints are engaged in prayer,
>> are engaged in fasts,
>> are engaged in the word,
>> are engaged within The Will of God.

The watchtowers of the saints work at releasing from the prisons,
>> work at restoring health,
>> work at increasing Faith,
>> work at creating testimonies,
>> work at the establishment of outposts,
>> work at the encouraging of The Disciples of The Lord.

The watchtowers of the saints are within The Edifice of God,

> are within the visions of The Saints,
> are within the reach of those who seek.
>
> The watchtowers of the saints know of a staircase to the heavens,
> a staircase to a home-coming,
> a staircase which can be mounted one step at
> a time,
> a staircase behind the door which is waiting for
> a knock."

My Content Study Aid

The Livery of God

"The livery of man is always open to inspection.

The livery of man is designed for inspection,
        is selected for inspection,
        is worn for inspection.

The livery of man is designed to make a mark,
        designed to impose a statement,
        designed to draw attention,
        designed to promote an entity.

The livery of man is designed for strutting,
        designed to create a bond,
        designed to be remembered,
        designed to enhance opinion,
        designed to cause a comment,
        designed to complement activity.

The livery of man is designed to emphasize a feature.

The livery of man is often maintained past its time of relevance.

The livery of man is often the cause of mirth,
        is often the cause of reflection,
        is often the cause of pride,
        is often the cause of envy,
        is often the cause of a fancy dress,
        is often the cause of glorying in the past.

The livery of man is not the livery of God.

The livery of God is not for the decision of man,
        is not for the decision of His servants,
        is not for the decision of the market place.

The livery of God is not for the decision of the devil.

The livery of God is not at the behest of the mockers,
        is not subject to the design of man,
        is not displayed where God remains unknown,
        is not brought before the saints where there are murmurs of dissent.

The livery of God unifies My Church,
        identifies the closeness of My Bride,
        is the mantle of My saints,
        is the sign for My people in The End-time troubling of man.

The livery of God is the footprint of the reality of God upon The Earth:
>is within the preparation for the coming King,
>is within the testimony of My saints preserved upon The Earth,
>is within The End-time prophecy of God,*
>is within My Banner from the distant islands of the seas,
>is within an emblem of My Spirit now brought upon The Earth.

The livery of God is within My Flag,
>is within My Standard,
>is within The Edifice of God.

The livery of God is a welcome sign to man:
>signifies a trysting place for My saints,
>signifies the past onset of reconciliation,
>signifies The Banner of My Kingdom instated by My Spirit.

The livery of God is a welcome sign to God,
>is a welcome sign from God,
>is a welcome sign of God.

The livery of God signs where Faith is present,
>signs where there is unity,
>signs where The New King is awaited.

The livery of God is seen upon His Earth."

* ***Scribal Note***: *Dictated Scripture index,*
Bible, (NKJV), Isaiah 52:13— as He selected, to 53:12. The Sin-Bearing Servant

Isa 52:13 Behold, My Servant shall deal prudently; He shall be exalted and extolled and be very high.

Isa 52:14 Just as many were astonished at you, So His visage was marred more than any man, And His form more than the sons of men;

Isa 52:15 So shall He sprinkle many nations. Kings shall shut their mouths at Him; For what had not been told them they shall see, And what they had not heard they shall consider.

Isa 53:1 Who has believed our report? And to whom has the arm of the LORD been revealed?

Isa 53:2 For He shall grow up before Him as a tender plant, And as a root out of dry ground. He has no form or comeliness; And when we see Him, There is no beauty that we should desire Him.

Isa 53:3 He is despised and rejected by men, A Man of sorrows and acquainted with grief. And we hid, as it were, our faces from Him; He was despised, and we did not esteem Him.

Isa 53:4 Surely He has borne our griefs And carried our sorrows; Yet we esteemed Him stricken, Smitten by God, and afflicted.

Isa 53:5 But He was wounded for our transgressions, He was bruised for our iniquities;

The chastisement for our peace was upon Him, And by His stripes we are healed.

Isa 53:6 All we like sheep have gone astray; We have turned, every one, to his own way; And the LORD has laid on Him the iniquity of us all.

Isa 53:7 He was oppressed and He was afflicted, Yet He opened not His mouth; He was led as a lamb to the slaughter, And as a sheep before its shearers is silent, So He opened not His mouth.

Isa 53:8 He was taken from prison and from judgment, And who will declare His generation? For He was cut off from the land of the living; For the transgressions of My people He was stricken.

Isa 53:9 And they made His grave with the wicked—But with the rich at His death, Because He had done no violence, Nor was any deceit in His mouth.

Isa 53:10 Yet it pleased the LORD to bruise Him; He has put Him to grief. When You make His soul an offering for sin, He shall see His seed, He shall prolong His days, And the pleasure of the LORD shall prosper in His hand.

Isa 53:11 He shall see the labor of His soul, and be satisfied. By His knowledge My righteous Servant shall justify many, For He shall bear their iniquities.

Isa 53:12 Therefore I will divide Him a portion with the great, And He shall divide the spoil with the strong, Because He poured out His soul unto death, And He was numbered with the transgressors, And He bore the sin of many, And made intercession for the transgressors.

Bible Commentary*: New Spirit Filled Life Bible, NKJV Variant, 52:13-53:12. Behold My Servant: This is the final servant Song. It is one of the greatest passages in the Bible, the mountain peak of Isaiah's book, the most sublime messianic prophecy in the OT, relating so many features of Jesus Christ's redemptive work. The song concerns the enemies' killing of the Servant (Messiah) (53:4, 5), who astonishingly is restored to life by Yahweh (53:10. All His suffering and His death are for others' sins (53:5).*

This text is also included in His Bk8: 'The Garden of The Cross',
'GOD Speaks of Loving His Creation'.

My Content Study Aid

_____
_____
_____
_____
_____
_____
_____

Emblem of The Spirit in Use

Embroidered Multi-fitting Caps   Screen-printed T-Shirts

For Team Sports, Youth Groups, Christian Activities, Get Togethers, Marches, Camps, Witnessing, Displays of Solidarity, Regional Games, Cycling, Recreational Day-wear.

Emblem of The Kingdom of God in Use

Self-Adhesive(peelable) Vinyl Decals
In two sizes as suited: 30x60mm or 70x140mm

*Make a Statement
Remind us of a Relationship
Start a Conversation*

Emblem of The Kingdom of God in Use

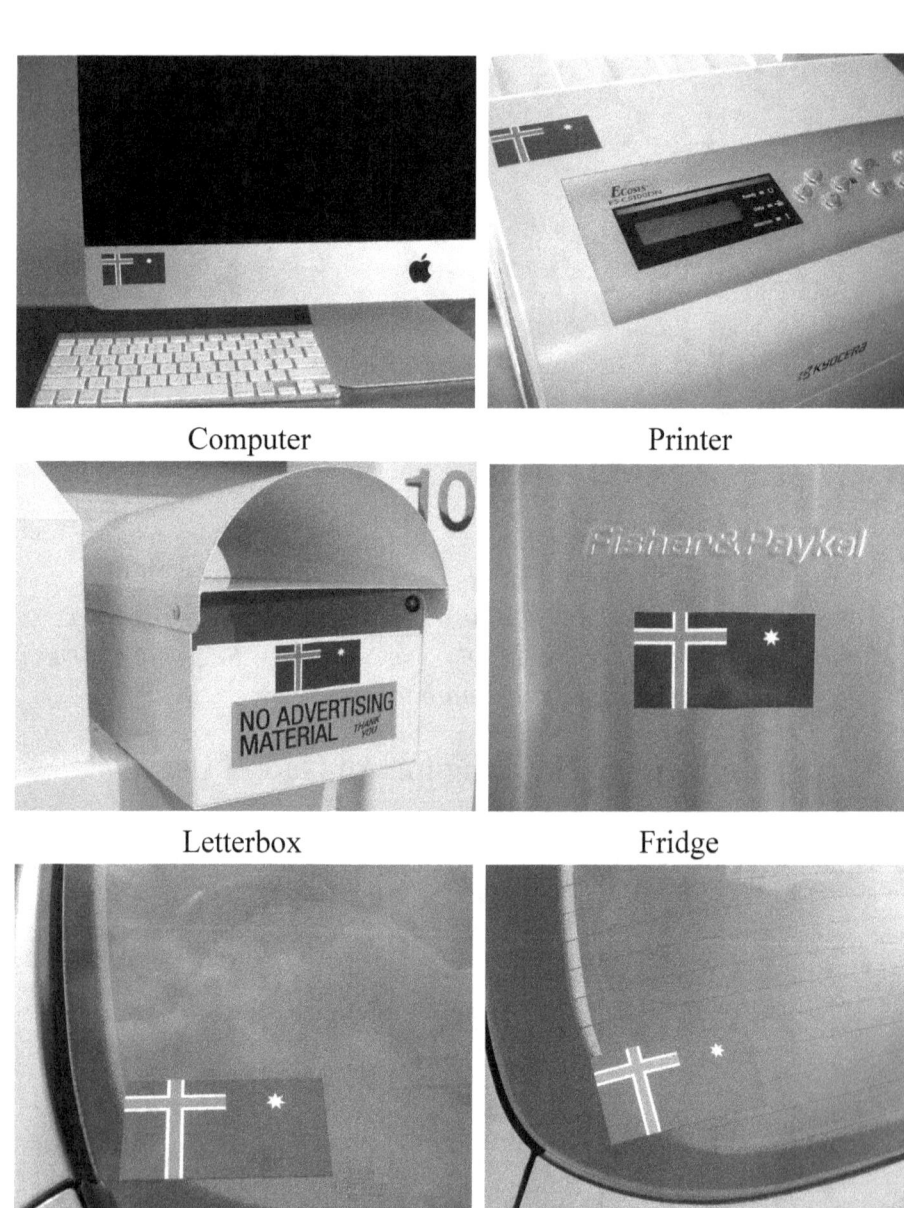

Computer

Printer

Letterbox

Fridge

Car Windscreen

Car Rear Window

Windows, Front Door, and many others—e.g. School books, Lunch Boxes.

The Days of Christmas

"The days of Christmas are the days of expectation for the young,
                 are the days of fulfilment for the families,
                 are the days of gratification for the elderly.

The days of Christmas signify man's rejoicing at a birth,
                 man's gathering in worship,
                 man's experience of love.

The days of Christmas signify the workload of the angels,
                 the workload of the mothers,
                 the workload of My servants.

The days of Christmas greet the completion of a circuit of the home of man.

The days of Christmas greet the sequences of the centuries,
                 greet happiness enthroned,
                 greet maturity explained with forgiveness attached.

The days of Christmas greet remembrance of the past,
                 greet the promise of the present,
                 greet the anticipation buried in the future.

The days of Christmas yield the blessings of God,
                 bring the sounds of glee,
                 carry the friendships of The Earth.

The days of Christmas ushered in the dawning of an age,
                 ushered in the planning for the wedding of The Bride,
                 ushered in the potential blessings presented in a child,
                 ushered in the introduction of The Bridegroom of man,
                 ushered in a lamb who would mingle with His flock,
                 ushered in cross-relationships between man and his God.

The days of Christmas brought applause to The Earth,
                 brought finality to a conquest,
                 brought companionship to man,
                 brought knowledge of the God of man in the wake of angels.

The days of Christmas brought the records of the prophets to the fore,
                 brought the prophecies of old into the reality of man,
                 brought The Son of Man to be as an effigy on a cross,
                 brought understanding of a sacrifice into the being of man,
                 brought grace personified into the grasp of man,
                 brought a future of freedom within the reach of man.

The days of Christmas led to an unfolding story,

        led to a homeward path,
        led to a focus of forgiveness,
        led to the spreading of great hope,
        led to the arguments of man,
        led to the fulfilment of the intent of God for man.

The days of Christmas reach out to all The Earth,
        vanquish the forces of dismay,
        water and sprout the seeds of Faith.

The days of Christmas are undergirded by The Faith of man,
        are undergirded by the God of action,
        are undergirded by the presence of My Spirit in the lives of man.

The days of Christmas are for the gathering of help,
        the gathering of assistance,
        the gathering of compassion for the estate of man.

The days of Christmas are the archetypes for man to bless his fellow man,
        for man to forgive his fellow man,
        for man to discern the need for a sacrificial
            offering for his fellow man.

The days of Christmas are to call to the poor in spirit,
        are to call to the poor in comfort,
        are to call to the poor who are yet to know their God—
            He who awaits within the wings."

My Content Study Aid

The Gratitude of Man

"Gratitude is not easily instilled in man,
        is often not expressed by man,
        is often not found within a culture,
        is often not encouraged by the parents,
        is often not heard within a family,
        is often not mentioned in a prayer,
        is often not inherent in a gift.

Gratitude can be the missing link to the unlocking of a heart,
                    to the meeting of a need,
                    to the answering of prayer,
                    to the presenting of a gift,
                    to the fellowship of man.

Gratitude can be the missing link to fellowship with God,
                      to a beacon in the sky which guides the angels,
                      to a beacon on The Earth which repels the demons,
                      to a beacon in a temple which confirms a guest
                                                        at home.

Gratitude is issued from within the heart of man,
    is a sign of well-being,
    is a sign of cleanliness,
    is a sign of a growing spirit,
    is a sign of a seeking soul with favour to the fore.

Gratitude is evident with a handshake of sincerity,
        with a mouth avoiding triteness of expression,
        with a written word espousing all which has gone before in easing
                                            the environment of man.

Gratitude is recognizable as a smile-enhancing attribute,
            as arising from a willing platform tendering assistance,
            as arising in response to a frantic call for help,
            as arising in the presence of an unexpected benefit,
            as arising from a service not rendered superficially,
            as arising from a pleasant surprise within the day,
            as arising from a measure deemed well in excess of
                                                          the minimum.

Gratitude is not offered for reward,
    is not tendered for recognition,
    is not sought as an entry standing as a record.

Gratitude is the namesake of appreciation:

       for the expression of a kindness,
       for thankfulness attributed where pride is not evident,
       for the granting of a favour with payment unexpected.

Gratitude rewards the giver and the thanker,
       the receiver and the offerer,
       the target and the sender.

Gratitude appears as anathema to the unforgiving,
    appears as a blessing to the humble,
    appears as a stumbling block to the proud,
    appears as gratuitous to the insincere,
    appears as wasted to the selfish,
    appears as a millstone round the neck of the self-centred.

Gratitude speaks of a grateful heart for what has been received,
    speaks of a loving spirit for what has been imparted,
    speaks of a soul appreciative of the counsel,
           of instruction,
           of the teaching:
                   as part of the offering from God.

Gratitude conveys a message straight from the heart of man to the heart of God.

Gratitude is the strengthener of the bonds of love.

Gratitude is the builder of a relationship with God.

Gratitude invigorates the spirit and the soul of man.

Gratitude is the heart throb of eternity,
    fills the well of life to overflowing,
    is as the anchor chain holding the ship of man in safety when at rest within
                                               a harbour.

The gratitude of man always is fully heard when in a discourse with The Father.

The gratitude of man always has attention when in the prayer time to The Son.

The gratitude of man always is conveyed when uttered in a tongue of My Spirit.

The gratitude of man always is well received by his loving God."

My Content Study Aid

_____
_____
_____
_____
_____

The Wiles of Woman

"The wiles of woman are underestimated by man,
　　　　　　　are the defences to authority,
　　　　　　　are the achievers of desire.

The wiles of woman are circuitous in their reasoning,
　　　　　　　are cunning in their plotting,
　　　　　　　are devious in their initiating.

The wiles of woman are devoted to strategize control,
　　　　　　　to the seizing of the day,
　　　　　　　to succeed against the odds.

The wiles of woman are there for the protection of her child,
　　　　　　　for the favouring of her family,
　　　　　　　for the progressing of her endeavours.

The wiles of woman are not open to inspection,
　　　　　　　do not appear in writing,
　　　　　　　vary with the circumstance.

The wiles of woman are a source of satisfaction,
　　　　　　　are a tribute to the process,
　　　　　　　are never subjected to a scene in haste.

The wiles of woman often find fulfilment in a mirror,
　　　　　　　fulfilment on an arm,
　　　　　　　fulfilment with a cradle.

The wiles of woman always are centred on a goal,
　　　　　　　always have a target,
　　　　　　　always are fixated on the objective of desire.

The wiles of woman improve with anxiety,
　　　　　　　improve with a trial,
　　　　　　　improve with a need.

The wiles of woman are present at a want,
　　　　　　　are present when acquiring,
　　　　　　　are present on reflection.

The wiles of woman are difficult to recognize,
　　　　　　　are difficult to counter,
　　　　　　　are difficult to negate.

The wiles of woman are not gracious in defeat.

The wiles of woman are seen in the end result,

> are seen upon completion,
> are seen upon achievement,
> are seen within the aura of success.

The wiles of woman is the armouring of God:
> is the empowering of woman,
> is the solution available to woman,
> is the tackling of a task where opposition is removed.

The wiles of woman should be known by man as they are known by God.

The wiles of woman are hidden when insecure,
> are disclosed when no longer relevant,
> are an anachronism of behaviour.

The wiles of woman are not drawn from within a pool,
> are drawn from deep within the soul.

The wiles of woman are not a function of the spirit,
> can involve the body,
> can offer understanding to the inexplicable.

The wiles of woman can explain the reasoning,
> can explain an outcome of surprise,
> can explain a change in mood,
> can explain a switching of attention,
> can explain becoming captive to a hobby,
> can explain a smile upon a face.

The wiles of woman are a function of the will,
> are a function of freewill in action,
> are a function designed to combat the imposition of subservience.

The wiles of woman are within the oversight of God."

My Content Study Aid

___
___
___
___
___
___
___
___

The Allergies of Man

"The allergies of man are bound in a single source,
                are found within a single cause,
                are wound upon a single spool.

The allergies of man expand and multiply in an environment without correction,
                          in an environment where the source is
                                        not identified,
                          in an environment where the solution is
                                        selected from a patchwork offering.

The allergies of man are free to come and go when only the symptoms are addressed,
                              when the root is left to thrive,
                              when the vine within the woods is only
                                        pruned and left in place.

The allergies of man are many and varied,
                are vicious and antagonistic,
                are anchored and can grow.

The allergies of man are parasitic in their nature,
                have varied fruits arising from the root,
                have a rootstock born of centuries,
                have varieties grafted on upon a whim.

The allergies of man are not for the benefit of man,
                are as the spewing to the surface of what is hidden in the depths,
                are the signs of man being used as a playground
                                in the absence of his knowledge,
                                in the absence of firmness of control,
                                in the presence of a trivial objection
                                        which is easily dismissed.

The allergies of man ride a seesaw of attention,
            gallop to the front,
            depart slowly to the rear,
            link hands in an attack,
            withdraw for a new stand.

The allergies of man thrive on the palliatives of man,
            thrive on the ignorance of man,
            thrive on the inaction of man,
            thrive on the complacency of man,
            thrive on the secularity of man,
            thrive on the acceptance of man.

The allergies of man cross the generations of man,
                cross the generations of inheritance,
                cross the generations where ignorance prevails,
                cross the generations to the detriment of man.

The allergies of man cause irritation to the life of man,
                bring termination to the life of man,
                bring fear with stress into the life of man.

The allergies of man are not dependent on the age of man within mortality.

The allergies of man bring dread into the quest for well-being,
                bring tears to the eyes of the loving,
                bring frustration to the seekers of solutions,
                bring consecutive rounds of testing,
                            of prodding,
                            of examining,
                            of swabbing—
                                        for what appear to have no end.

The allergies of man are not superficial in appearance,
                are not superficial in the causes,
                are not superficial in effects,
                are not superficial in the results,
                are not superficial in their nature,
                are not superficial when formulating the process of recovery.

The allergies of man require the full attention of man,
                require extensive preparation,
                require a time-table set for confrontation,
                require knowledge of the past,
                require access to assistance,
                require surety of completion.

The allergies of man require single-mindedness of purpose,
                require fervency of intent,
                require the utterances of resolve.

The allergies of man concede,
                vacate,
                disperse,
                            in the presence of the servants prepared for battle—
                                        with appointments to the day.

The allergies of man can be made to pack their bags and leave,
                can be made the invaders subject to defeat,
                can be made to ensure the dwelling is fit for habitation.

The allergies of man do not have permanence of tenure,

    do not have the ability to resist eviction in the face of
            unwavering determination,
    do not have authority to stay when met head-on by the binding
          power of knowledge applied with wisdom.

The allergies of man can create mayhem in the health of man,
    can create doubt of the effectiveness of The Cross,
    can create an estranged walk with God.

The allergies of man need to be vanquished from a venue,
    need to be castigated for the imposing of their will—
            where it is not welcome,
    need to be forbidden to return.

The allergies of man obey the promise of The Cross,
    obey the servants with authority which supersedes the foe of man,
    obey the firestorm invoked as The Refiner's fire,
    obey the firestorm which advances against the foe of man.

The allergies of man are curses rendered down the generations of man,
    are out-workings of demonic influence,
    are invasive in the absence of a firewall built upon the rock.

The allergies of man cannot surmount the firewall of great height,
    cannot burrow through a non-existent crack,
    cannot access a circular enclosure,
    cannot tunnel under the foundations built of jasper*,
          of emeralds*,
          of the canon of the word.

The allergies of man must not be allowed to build upon the permissions granted in
            the past,
      to stake their claims upon inheritance,
      to gather at the frontiers of passivity,
      to strengthen the acceptance of their presence,
      to develop the influencing of a soul,
      to impact upon the spirit's plight.

The allergies of man are not an end unto themselves,
    are not permanent in their fixtures,
    can be thrown out with the rubbish.

The allergies of man are not inherent features in the being of man,
    are not permissive features within the landscape set by God,
    are not features set by a loving God to bring suffering to the life
            of man.

The allergies of man arise from the voyeurs of iniquity,
    from those who would gaze upon the inflicted with smiles

>of satisfaction,
from those who build on the opportunities arising from
the past.

The allergies of man need to be dealt with for what they are,
must not be misdiagnosed if release is to be attained,
must not be treated lightly as if a touch of sunburn between
the clouds,
must not be ignored in the belief they will go away.

The allergies of man are rampant,
are extensive,
are prolonged,
are painful,
are disfiguring,
are distorting,
are inflicting,
are crippling.

The allergies of man are often bound to the food of man,
are often targeted at the senses of man,
are often aligned to the surroundings of man.

The allergies of man are not contagious on discovery,
are self-erasing on dismissal,
do not mount repetitive attempts at later reinstatement.

The allergies of man are of concern to God,
are within The Wisdom of My servants,
are within the matters dealt with at The Cross,
are within the validity of prayers submitted to the heavens—
for action on The Earth,
are within the binding and the loosing—
in freeing either the body or The Temple for life within its fullness."

* *Scribal Note:* *Refer to* Divine Commentary on the Book of Revelation 21:19,
His Book 2: 'GOD Speaks to Man On The Internet'

My Content Study Aid

_____
_____
_____
_____
_____

The Visitation of India

"The visitation of India is not lightly undertaken,
        is not for the unprepared,
        is not for the insensitive.

The visitation of India is to confirm My Spirit's call,
        is to confirm a raft of reasons,
        is to confirm the paddling of a boat.

The visitation of India is timed within a station,
        is timed within the families,
        is timed within the arrangements known to God.

The visitation of India is specific and precise,
        is abundant and rewarding,
        is surprised and grateful.

The visitation of India is not to bring objections from My servants,
        is not to bring a recall of My servants,
        is not to bring irateness to a face.

The visitation of India is to enhance the lives of My people—
              those who come,
              those who go,
              those who live and stay in India.

The visitation of India is not experienced by all My servants.
The visitation of India is a blessing from The Lord.
The visitation of India is a blessing for My people there."

My Content Study Aid

The Enquiring of My Spirit

"The enquiring of My Spirit is available to all who live in Faith,
        is available to all with a commitment,
        is available to all with a testimony,
        is available to all receiving the offer of My Grace.

The enquiring of My Spirit affirms the reality of relationship,
        is the threshold to a conversation,
        results in knowledge imparted to and fro,
        adds to an experience within the life of man.

The enquiring of My Spirit is a benchmark in man's walk with God.

The enquiring of My Spirit invites the tendering of an answer,
        invites a response which stands the test of time,
        invites the bringing forth of knowledge wrapped in wisdom.

The enquiring of My Spirit is the thirsting for counsel from divinity,
        is the seeking for The Will of God,
        is the having of confirmation of being within the earshot of
                      The Lord.

The enquiring of My Spirit is always welcomed by God;
        is always attended to by God;
        is always ready for,
        is always available to,
        is always keyed for ready access by:
                the utterances of man—
        whether of The Earth or whether of the heavens.

The enquiring of My Spirit is at the onset of two-way communication:
                with The I AM of creation,
                with The I AM of the heavens,
                with The I AM of The Earth,
                with The I AM of man.

The enquiring of My Spirit is not for the frivolous or the immaterial,
        is neither as an oracle nor as a satisfier of curiosity,
        is not for the soothsayer,
        is not for a séance,
        is not for the mysteries of God.

The enquiring of My Spirit may be sought for a word of knowledge,
        for a word of wisdom—
        for a word which has relevance when
            immersed in a battle to free the soul of man.

The enquiring of My Spirit is the call of My servant seeking direction
        on how best to extend The Kingdom of God,
        on how best to pray for the healing of affliction,
        on how best to bless the broken-hearted,
        on how best to deal with curses,
        on how best to bring freedom from idolatry.

The enquiring of My Spirit may be sought for interpretation arising
        from My Spirit's tongues:
        from the speaking of My Spirit's tongues;
        from the hearing of My Spirit's tongues.

The enquiring of My Spirit may be sought for translation:
        arising from the tongues of man into My Spirit's tongues;
        arising from My Spirit's tongues into the tongues of man.

The enquiring of My Spirit signifies access within The Will of God,
        access to the healing will of God,
        access to the uplifting power of God,
        access to the overcoming knowledge for dealing
                with the demons,
        access to the underlying knowledge which
                enhances lives.

The enquiring of My Spirit is a blessing reserved unto My servants,
        is a blessing which discloses what should be bound or loosed
                so a status may be changed,
        is a blessing of effectiveness in the ministry of God,
        is a blessing of achievement in the ministering of My servants
                to the peoples of The Earth.

The enquiring of My Spirit accompanies the extended ability to speak an extensive range
        of My Spirit's tongues.

The enquiring of My Spirit follows The Fear of The Lord,
        follows The Wisdom of God,
        follows familiarity with both the gifts and the tongues of
                My Spirit.

The enquiring of My Spirit follows a close relationship with God."

My Content Study Aid

_____

_____

_____

The Wailing of The Innocent

"The wailing of the innocent is always heard by God.
The wailing of the innocent is the loudest cry on Earth.
The wailing of the innocent is of compassion for the distraught.

The wailing of the innocent is the scream of much desperation,
                is the cry of much pain,
                is the outpouring of much grief.

The wailing of the innocent is not a pleasant sound,
                disturbs all who hear it,
                upsets all who view it,
                dismays all unable to bring comfort.

The wailing of the innocent puts a searchlight on the scene,
                puts a spotlight on the reason,
                puts a footlight on the victim,
                puts a torch light on the happenings of the day.

The wailing of the innocent puts a floodlight on the background to that which brought
                                                                                    it forth.

The wailing of the innocent is not drawn out for effect,
                is not drawn out to gather sympathy,
                is not drawn out to point a finger.

The wailing of the innocent is not a guide light to the source of such distress,
                is not an array of noise which brings distraction,
                is as a lighthouse in the darkness which has lost its light.

The wailing of the innocent is dependent on discernment of the spirit,
                        on internment with the spirit,
                        on refinement by the spirit.

The wailing of the innocent is quietened by concern,
                is quietened by assistance,
                is quietened by companionship.

The wailing of the innocent is silenced by release,
                is silenced by belief,
                is silenced by attention.

The wailing of the innocent is rewarded by the onset of hope,
                      by the onset of Faith,
                      by the onset of the truth.

The wailing of the innocent is rewarded by the onset of trust,

>   by the onset of freedom,
>   by the onset of a life regained.

The wailing of the innocent is occasioned by the lies,
>   is occasioned by lack of care,
>   is occasioned by a verdict brought by man.

The wailing of the innocent occasions the onset of paralysis,
>   the onset of restrictions,
>   the onset of captivity.

The wailing of the innocent occasions the continuation of the prayers.

The wailing of the innocent calls for a revision of that which brought it forth.

The wailing of the innocent is a signal for appeal.

The wailing of the innocent is confirmed by God.

The wailing of the innocent calls for a righting of a wrong,
>   calls for perseverance,
>   calls for mobilization of righteousness infringed.

The wailing of the innocent is still heard by God when within the thrall of silence,
>   when in a paroxysm of intent,
>   when distanced by adversity,
>   when subjected to correction,
>   when summoned by authority,
>   when vacated by the relatives who are
>   reserved to care.

The wailing of the innocent is not always heard for what it is,
>   can be misinterpreted by man,
>   can be discarded as the emotion of the moment,
>   can be known to children,
>   can be misapplied by the servants of the courts of man.

The wailing of the innocent is often heard at the full-stop of a sentence—
>   when there is a call for a setting of example,
>   when publicity has crucified the just to the making of a story,
>   when there is no repentance from the secret doubters who
>   still brought it so to be.

The wailing of the innocent tugs at the hearts which still live and question,
>   which still study and derive,
>   which still test and validate—
>   what has gone before.

The wailing of the innocent is as a long-lived call arising from injustice:
>   which besets the soul of man with the cry of ages,
>   'Father,
>   forgive them for they know not what they do.' "

Righteousness

"Righteousness is a prerequisite for entry into the presence of God.

Righteousness enables trust within the truth.

Righteousness prevails against the intent of evil.

Righteousness is the source of a relationship with God.

Righteousness surmounts the temptations of depravity,
                the temptations of iniquity,
                the temptations of debauchery,
                the temptations of dishonesty,
                the temptations of deceit,
                the temptations of idolatry,
                the temptations of man deemed by God as sin.

Righteousness is built on Faith,
        is anchored on Faith,
        is established on Faith.

  For as righteousness exists within the character
                      so it is ascribed as measured within the soul.

  For as righteousness calibrates the influence of the spirit
                      so the soul is plumbed to the depth ascribed.

  For as righteousness surmounts the mountaintop of Faith
                      so sin is vanquished from The Temple ascribed to God.

Righteousness is the backbone of existence,
        is the central concept within a life,
        is the keynote of exploration,
        is the harbinger of peace.

Righteousness walks hand in hand with God.

Righteousness does not straddle a fence of separation,
        does not promote a shadow,
        does not frequent the shade.

Righteousness is a companion to The Son light,
        is a companion to The Spirit's counsel,
        is inherent in The Father's outlook.

Righteousness is an acquisition of the soul,
        is an attribute of the justice of Divinity,
        is a requirement issuing from the throne room of God.

Righteousness imparts strength into a character,

        imparts strength to withstand temptation,
        imparts strength to deflect the fiery darts of demons.

Righteousness is not kindled in the spirit,
        is not transmitted to the soul,
        is not manifested by the body:
              by the pursuance of the temptations of man.

Righteousness imparts knowledge to pursue The Wisdom which enables access to the counselling of God.

Righteousness is achievable through Faith,
        is achievable through freewill,
        is achievable by a mindset of repentance,
            a mindset of forgiveness,
            a mindset of commitment,
            a mindset which walks the morality of God.

Righteousness develops in a storyline of truth which rests upon a life as it learns the ways of God.

Righteousness develops as a life changes the contents of its shopping,
            of what it carries home,
            of what it chooses to consume,
            of what it then discards as bitter to the tongue.

Righteousness follows the cleaning of a house,
        the forsaking of idolatry,
        the disposing of the dross which is not transmitted through the fire.

Righteousness abounds within The Temple known to God,
        is secure when cared for by The Spirit of God,
        is protected when subjected to an unwise decision in the presence of God.

Righteousness is essential in the preparation of The Bride,
        in the being of The Bride,
        in the qualifying of The Bride.

Righteousness is at the forefront of discussion:
            in the selection of The Bride,
            in the encouraging of The Bride,
            in the rejection of those who have delayed their preparation beyond the day of man.

Righteousness is not hidden in a stoppered bottle pending its release;
        is not awaiting at the summit of a mountain built of glass and ice;
        is not dependent on a list of do's and don'ts;
        is not a substance of the senses which puts a burden on a back;

        is not the acquiring of a password which guarantees success;
        is not the sequencing of activities which builds a rope to Heaven.

Righteousness is not proclaimed by man,
        is not fettered by the freewill of man,
        is not achieved by those without commitment.

Righteousness affects the heart of man,
        affects the welfare of man,
        affects the future of man,
        affects the compassion of the love of man,
        affects what becomes the centre of the affection of man,
        affects the willingness of man to serve.

Righteousness is the gate which is opened by The Spirit of God in the presence of the
                                                        Faith of man:
                as Faith so dwells within the soul of man.

Righteousness has no weight to carry,
        brings joy with exhilaration,
        settles a life with clarity of perspective,
                with understanding of the purpose,
                with fulfilment bound within a new covenant in force."

My Content Study Aid

India is A Land

"India is a land set for refreshing,
    is a land set for My Spirit's call,
    is a land within the sway of demons,
    is a land without a throne,
    is a land ruled by the idolatrous,
        by the selfish,
        by the uncaring,
        by the corrupt,
        by the inept—
            by those who prepare to paint the future with the brushstrokes of
                      the present—
                      to the detriment of all.

India is a land set for the reigning of My Spirit,
    is a land set for the giftings of My Spirit,
    is a land set for the blooming of the flowers of God,
    is a land set for the raising of the righteous,
    is a land set for the prophets' calls,
        set for the prophets' messages,
        set for the declarations from The Loving God.

India is a land set for the tending of My servants,
    so it may know the verdancy of the rice fields,
    so it may know the roads of travelling,
    so it may know the produce of renown,
    so it may share its wealth among its people,
    so the learned and the wise will be instated with authority,
    so the aged and the infirm will turn from cursing into blessing,
    so the young may see the promise of procurement overlay the curse of desolation,
    so the labourer and the artisan may both be rewarded for the effort of the day,
    so the captains of industry will share willingly with their staff so all
                              may be enriched,
                              content,
                              at peace—
            as righteousness prevails upon the land of India.

India is set to be an example to The Multitudes who can neither read nor write,
                        who are enslaved by their mother tongues,
                        who cannot prescribe the plans which meet
                                  their aspirations.

India is a land set with peoples waiting to be freed.

India is a land deserving to be freed

        from the necessity for corruption,
        from the circumstances inviting greed,
        from the implications stemming from a lack of education,
        from a lack of interest in the welfare of the people,
        from an incentive,
            to treat the people with the honour and the integrity due each
                    soul upon The Earth.

India is a land awaiting the breaking of the classes for the prospering of all,
        awaiting the updating of the facilities which enhance each
                life encountered,
        awaiting the fair trading of communities which validate a family
                with security:
                    of expectation;
                    of shelter;
                    of sustenance.

India is a land waiting for a vision which can usher in a land of plenty to all who
                dwell therein.

India is a land awaiting a re-awakening so the promised future may be uplifted
                as fit for all.

India is a land of history,
    is a land of capabilities,
    is a land of complacency,
    is a land of inequality,
    is a land oppressed by those who rule only in self-interest—
                yet shelter behind the petticoats of democracy:
                that which it was not intended ever to describe."

My Content Study Aid

My Servants in India

"My servants sow the seeds of signs and wonders in the land of India.

My servants impress the need for righteousness,
        the need for heartfelt prayer,
        the need to be fixated
                as a dog is on a bone,
                as a goal is kept within the sight of day,
                as a target for ardent prayer is nurtured in much Faith.

My servants are at the forefront of the outreach of My Spirit,
        are not expected to lag behind,
        are not casually positioned,
        are not deafened to a need,
        are not forsaken by My Spirit's call.

My servants are at the reaping of the harvest,
        are at the attending of the annunciations of My Spirit,
        are the vehicles of transmission of My word,
                of The Wisdom of My Spirit,
                of the knowledge there imparted at
                        a divine appointment.

My servants are the carts behind the bullocks,
        the wagons behind the water buffalo,
        the followers of the sentinel who lights the placing of their feet.

My servants know the blessings of My Spirit,
        know to wield My word with substance and with Grace,
        know to hearken to My Spirit as counsellor and affirmer,
        know to pray within The Will of God,
        know the need to have familiarity with The Will of God,
        know how to seek,
        know how to declare,
        know how to loose and bind.

My servants know how to fulfill the expectations God has for His servants.

My servants know The Faith which calls down the fire of Heaven—
            to thereby bring the warmth of healing to My people—
            to thereby remove demonic influences—
            to thereby instate the tongues of Heaven—
            to thereby announce the very presence of the God of Love—
            to thereby create a testimony of the God who seeks involvement
                              in their lives.

My servants know The Faith which does not waver,
>   The Grace which does not depart,
>   the gifts which are not withdrawn.

My servants know the reality of that of which they share,
>   the being as the reason for their presence,
>   the authority with the signs and wonders as God upholds His word,
>>   His servants,
>>   His Spirit,
>>   before the face of man.

My servants have their trust firmly embedded in the integrity of God,
>   in the power displayed which defies the explanations of man,
>   in the miracles encountered within the healing power of God,
>   in the upholding of The Will of God as spoken by His servants,
>   in the uplifting by The Will of God with both the knowledge
>>   and The Wisdom of His servants bound in Faith."

My Content Study Aid

The Benevolence of Grace

"The benevolence of grace is offered freely without recourse for sin,
        is offered freely from a heart of perfect love,
        is offered freely so man need not fear the law.

The benevolence of grace is offered freely to the open heart.

The benevolence of grace is offered freely to man in his mortality,
        to man while still a sinner,
        to man while still estranged from God,
        to man while still a felon awaiting judgment.

The benevolence of grace is offered freely to every soul,
        is awaiting acceptance of the offer,
        is the decider of the fate of man.

The benevolence of grace is offered freely as it lies,
        as fare upon a table,
        for the partaking of man.

The benevolence of grace is offered freely,
        as announced,
        for the attention of man.

The benevolence of grace is offered freely—
        in the best interests of man—
        an offer the soul of man is unwise to decline.

The benevolence of grace is offered freely,
        as the ultimate,
        in a loving covenant issuing from God."

My Content Study Aid

_____

_____

_____

_____

_____

_____

The Tongues of Heaven

"The tongue of man can speak the languages of The Earth,
          can speak the languages of the heavens,
          can speak the languages of Hell.

The tongue of man can vocalize the tongues of The Earth,
          can vocalize the tongues of the heavens,
          can vocalize the tongues of Hell.

The tongues of Earth can be interpreted by man.

The tongues of Heaven can be interpreted by My Spirit.

The tongues of Hell can be marshalled by demonic forces,
          can be installed by demonic forces.

The tongue of man signals intent to display all of his emotions—
          whether to his shame or to his honour,
                    to display all of his fears—
          whether real or imagined,
                    to display his heart's intent—
          whether as a home for righteousness or as what has been
                    surrendered to be then filled with evil.

The tongue of man has the ability of commissioning speech,
          of bringing forth commands,
          of instigating tears,
          of giving cause for smiles,
          of emitting an emotion which changes an expression
                    on a face.

The tongue of man can be sharp or soft,
          can be brief or loquacious,
          can be offensive or forgiving,
          can be surly or gracious.

The tongue of man rarely knows the need for silence,
          rarely has the time to put the ears to work:
          rarely has the ability to do both of these together.

The tongue of man requires the consent of Heaven to converse in the tongues of Heaven:
                    with or without the understanding of man.

The consent of Heaven is given as a gift of My Spirit in stages of ascent–
                    as they are sought,
                    as they are acquired,
                    as they are put to use,

as they are practised with intent.

The tongue of man when conversing in the tongues of Heaven is as if in a field filled
with wondrous explorations.

The tongues of Heaven can forge a channel of two-way communication within the
thought processes of man.

The tongues of Heaven can alter the thresholds and the sensors of the six senses of man.

The tongues of Heaven can translate the tongue of man into a tongue of man upon the
utterance of the day.

The tongues of Heaven reside within a multiplicity of selections,
    can be selected at the will of man,
    can be spoken at the will of man,
    can be thought at the will of man,
    can be transmitted at the will of man.

The tongues of Heaven are gifted by My Spirit to again dwell upon the tongue of man as
man is invited to prepare for the
end-time of the cavalcade of Grace.

The tongues of Heaven are gifted by My Spirit,
    in extensions,
    to fulfil the communicating abilities of man.

The tongues of Heaven can surmount the falsity of teachings which endeavour to explain
their age-long non-appearance
within the experience of man.

The tongues of Heaven are a blessing which will not intrude
    when they are not sought,
    when they are regarded as unnecessary,
    when their absence is taken as confirmation of their
non-relevance,
    when they are seen as being without value,
        as being without application,
        as being beyond the comprehension of man.

So it is common that the ignorant decline the misunderstood blessings of God.

So it is abounding that the wise avidly seek the blessings of God.

So the ignorant display their non-reading of My word wherein My apostles,
    Paul included,
    relay their familiarity,
        their experience,
    with My Spirit's gift of tongues:
    for the benefit both of My people,
    and as a sign to The Multitudes,
    of The Living God."

The Holiness of God

The Holiness of God does not dwell among the babble of man,
        does not dwell among The Multitudes of man,
          does not dwell in the outpourings of the requests of man.

The Holiness of God is a place of fear,
        is a place of intense communion,
          is a place where Abba and agapé are fully understood.

The Holiness of God cannot be breached by the will of man,
        cannot be usurped by evil,
          cannot be approached from a basis of idolatry.

The Holiness of God is not a venue for the complacent of heart and spirit,
        for the looseness of the tongue of man,
          for the shallow waters barely to the ankles of man.

The Holiness of God instates ongoing dialogue in the closest of relationships,
        presents The Will of God where it will not be ignored,
        sanctifies a soul with the assent of God.

The Holiness of God is for My servants prepared and equipped
                to approach,
                to converse with,
                to hear and to listen to,
                to wait upon,
                the very presence of their God.

The Holiness of God has no cause for the fear of man,
        does not call for the retreat of man,
        does not invite where uncleanliness prevents.

The Holiness of God does not recognize
          a heart intending to repent,
          a heart which lingers near a dustbin,
          a heart which knows the waste waters of past bathing.

The Holiness of God tracks those who are instilled with the discipleship of
                            The Holy Spirit,
          who have modified their walk,
          who have acknowledged their mistakes,
          who have sought and used the gifts of God within the
                            will of God.

The Holiness of God blesses in disclosing the open door of His Spirit's tongues."

The Foundation of My Kingdom

"The foundation of My Kingdom,
  the building of My Kingdom,
    the caring for The Edifice of God on Earth—
        is in the hands of My servants who labour in My vineyard.

The foundation of My Kingdom which is everlasting in its nature withstands the fire
                                                                     of testing.

The foundation of My Kingdom which is vanquished by the loss of Faith crumbles in
                                                                    the dust—
                              so fails the test of fire.

The foundation of My Kingdom is The Word of God proclaimed in truth,
                                      in righteousness,
                                      in The Fear of God.

The foundation of My Kingdom is built on with the gold of Faith,
                                the silver of Grace,
                                the precious stones of souls.

The foundation of My Kingdom is built on with the presence of My Spirit.
The foundation of My Kingdom may be added to by man.
The foundation of My Kingdom may be built on by man in the absence of My Spirit.
The foundation of My Kingdom*
        may be built on with wood which later rots—
                with doctrine which is false;
      may be built on with hay attacked by the mildew of decay—
                with paucity of the recognition of My Spirit;
      may be built on with straw which does not hold a vision—
                with the perishing of man.

  For such as these,
        the mistaken efforts of man:
        will bring no credit to his soul,
        will bring no recognition for his labours,
        will not prevail upon appeal,
        will not survive as an intended blessing,
        will not be present on the gown of life,
        will not be counted as treasure stored beyond the grave.

For such as these are fodder for the fire of righteousness—
    which tests the gifts of man for integrity of purpose:
        for that which will stand before the throne of God."

Scribal Note:
　　*The Bible, New King James version, 1 Corinthians 3:12-13
[12] Now if anyone builds on this foundation with gold, silver, precious stones, wood, hay, straw, [13] each one's work will become clear; for the Day will declare it, because it will be revealed by fire; and the fire will test each one's work, of what sort it is.

My Content Study Aid

The Days of Leanness

"The days of feasting are about to end on The Earth.

The days of feasting have fed the gluttony of man,
        the greed of man,
        the waist of man.

The days of feasting have not been shared with those dwelling
                under deprivation,
                under need,
                under the conflict of the nations.

The days of feasting will call to accountability all those seated at the table as a cartel
                of acrimony:
        all those who used a veto to frustrate
                the rest,
        all those who refused consent to share,
        all those who put their grossness of
                self-interest above the
                leanness of their fellow man.

The days of feasting decline into the days of leanness.

The days of leanness are about to bring hoarding to the fore,
        to bring escalating prices,
        to bring exceeding wealth to the poor in the absence
                of corruption.

The days of leanness are for the benefit of the sleeping nations,
            those awaiting their time within the sunshine,
            those who shall not be further plundered for
                the gain of the selfish few.

The days of leanness bring water to the arid lands,
        bring water to the frozen lands,
        bring water in abundance so these lands may bloom in the
                flowering of their season.

The days of leanness see a change in the trade winds of The Earth,
        see a change in the herbage of The Earth,
        see a change in the seas of The Earth.

The days of leanness see shrinkage from the lapping of the seas,
        see feeding patterns change across The Earth,
        see disasters aplenty in the domiciles of man,
        see the onslaught of the storming of The Earth.

The righteousness of God will prevail upon The Earth in the face of man."

The Storming of The Seas

"The storming of the seas leave no shore unwashed,
        leave scars on the memory of man,
        leave forlornness in the wake,
        leave the stranded on higher ground,
        leave the shorelines in the tatters of the day,
        leave the wreckage of man scattered for display.

The storming of the seas boil with the variance of disparity,
        vanquish the impediments encountered,
        demolish the constructions built for serving man,
        inundate the seizures of the day,
        release the targets for destruction,
        obfuscate the power of recognition.

The storming of the seas are general in the approach,
        do not harbour feelings of revenge,
        do not encircle so to crush,
        do not have the control of man,
        do not perform an encore,
        do not favour a time of day.

The storming of the seas terrify with their presence,
        threaten the safety of all,
        are the subject of much prayer,
        escalate to a crescendo,
        slide into oblivion,
        waken somewhere else on another day.

The storming of the seas surge far inland,
        exhibit force within the onslaught,
        gather to possess as their will decides,
        retreat with the looting of the day,
        dispose far and wide as the crest dictates,
        demonstrate the miracles of mercy on the surfaces of the seas.

The storming of the seas have a beginning and an end,
        encompass the futility of action too long delayed,
        reward the preparations needed for the day,
        succumb to the watchmen in the towers,
        circumvent the sentries on the battlements,
        signify a sanctuary to the perceptive and the righteous.

The storming of the seas overcome the vessels deployed upon the seas,
        turn to flotsam the craft within the harbours,

remove landscapes from the maps of man,
target for subjugation the monoliths of the day,
upheave the waters of invasions,
install the walls which teeter on the brink of the imaginings
of man.

The storming of the seas are the assaults on man,
on all his senses,
on his well-being,
on his security,
on his livelihood,
on his mortality of the day,
on his fragility of being.

The storming of the seas arise from the implications of the idolatry of man,
arise from man's appointment with the Kingdom,
arise from the blasphemies of man,
arise from the approaching of the day,
arise from the new covenant about to flower,
arise from The Holy Spirit's call,
arise from the declaration of the fullness of time."

My Content Study Aid

The Idolatry of Man

"The idolatry of man varies within each land,
      within each nation,
      within each tongue of the people,
      within each culture of man.

The idolatry of man is widespread,
    increasing by the day,
    bringing blasphemy of the tongue as the companion of the fool.

The idolatry of man expands with the opportunities before his eyes,
            before his ears,
            before his nose,
            before his mouth,
            before his hands,
            before his heart.

The idolatry of man is dependent on his senses.

The idolatry of man leads the soul without a care,
    leads the spirit with reluctance,
    leads the sinner without honour to the destiny of default.

The idolatry of man fixates to steal his time,
    fixates to steal his wealth,
    fixates to garner his attention,
    fixates on the hay or straw,
    fixates on gathering the fuel for testing with a fire.

The idolatry of man has worship which is ineffectual;
    has praise which is unacknowledged,
    has prayers which are ignored,
    has offerings of great expense,
    has disciples declaring the will of man as if The Will of God,
    has constructions which abjure The Living God.

The idolatry of man funnels man away from The God of truth with light,
            The God of life with love,
            The God of goodness with Grace.

The idolatry of man confirms man's fallen state,
    confirms man's walk in pride,
    confirms man's preoccupation with himself,
    confirms man's leading as by a ring within his nose,
    confirms man's captivity in the domain of Satan,
    confirms man's lack of perception in the gods he has established.

The idolatry of man soothes the frustrations of man,
                soothes the burdens of man,
                soothes the urgency of man,
                soothes the searching of man,
                soothes the inhibitions of man,
                soothes the objectives of man.

The idolatry of man soothes the expectations of man,
                soothes the acceptance of the counterfeit,
                soothes the wariness of the spirit,
                soothes the acceptability of lies,
                soothes the objections to the intent of evil,
                soothes the breaking of a promise.

The idolatry of man soothes man's search for God,
                soothes the destiny of default,
                soothes the beliefs of the agnostic,
                soothes the forbidden under God,
                soothes the word of God,
                soothes the truth for acceptance of deceit.

The idolatry of man soothes man in justifying the breaking of a heart within the presence of God.

The idolatry of man knows the impugning of righteousness in Faith,
                the clutching at a straw in hope,
                the ignoring of a life-boat sent when in distress.

The idolatry of man is a ploy of Satan,
                is a folly with immensity of effect,
                is the denigration of the truth,
                is the substitution which steals a destiny with The Living God."

My Content Study Aid

The Storm of Satan

"The storm of Satan is the composite of evil,
        is the high water of his reach,
        is the high point of the invasion of the will of man,
        is the manifested evil as infecting the souls of man,
        is the saga of the ages—
            the warring of the ages—
            coming to a rampant head.

The storm of Satan secretes its jurisdiction within the heart of man,
        secretes its objectives within the demons of attack,
        secretes its strategies within the strongholds at the gates.

The storm of Satan has pursuits for the souls who crave salaciousness;
                corruption;
                iniquities;
                violence;
        murder in all its descriptive killings—
                genocide,
                democide,
                policide,
                gendercide,
                androcide,
                femicide,
                tyrannicide,
                homicide,
                familicide,
                avunculicide,
                nepoticide,
                uxoricide,
                filicide,
                patricide,
                matricide,
                fratricide,
                sororicide,
                prolicide,
                infanticide,
                neonaticide,
                feticide,
                suicide—
        the killings originating from man in his forms of manslaughter:
            in his forms so named and used by man;
                harmfulness;

                              idolatry;
                              theft;
                              envy,
                              jealousy;
                              perversion in all its many forms:
                those designed to defame the being—
                                        the purpose—
                                                  of man.

The storm of Satan is the summiting of evil,
        the seal of hate for God,
        the battlefield for the souls of man.

The storm of Satan manifests the peaking of ill will to man,
        manifests the debauchery of man,
        manifests man uninhibited by his soul,
        manifests man as the voyeur of the age,
        manifests man forsaking self-control,
        manifests man at the low point of his fall.

The storm of Satan precedes his being taken into custody to serve a term of
                                                            one thousand years.

The storm of Satan precedes the coming of The King.

The storm of Satan precedes the climax of the storm—
                unleashes evil in its end-time fullness,
                unleashes evil in all its horrors on the children,
                unleashes evil in all its horrors on the mothers,
                unleashes evil in all its horrors on the wives,
                unleashes evil in all its horrors on the daughters,
                unleashes evil in all its horrors on the battlefield of Satan,
                unleashes evil in all its horrors on those who did not flee,
                        on those without a sanctuary,
                        on those who carried ineffectual arms,
                        on those who fought in ignorance
                                without the weapons,
                                without the knowledge,
                                without the wisdom to
                                      attain the victory.

The storm of Satan is linked to the storm of man:
                occurs as in the linking of the arms;
                displays in commonality of purpose;
                professes the descent of man in the absence of the
                                        morality of God.

The storm of Satan plays with the ethics of man founded in their relativity within the
unbridled soul.

The storm of Satan encourages the vengeance of man,
        encourages the quest for conquest,
        encourages the discarding of all righteousness,
        encourages the refighting of the wars of man,
        encourages the enmity of neighbours,
        encourages violence in the settling of disputes.

The storm of Satan is short-lived in extent,
        is barbarous in intent,
        is barbaric in its nature.

The storm of Satan foreshadows the end of the curséd Earth,
        the death knell of the curséd Earth,
        the completion of the age of Grace on the curséd Earth.

With the abatement of the storm of Satan comes the lifting of the curse upon The Earth,
        comes the age of enlightenment,
        comes the reigning of The King,
        comes righteousness with peace upon
The Earth of God."

My Content Study Aid

_____
_____
_____
_____
_____
_____
_____
_____
_____
_____
_____
_____
_____
_____
_____
_____
_____
_____

The Storm of Man

"The storm of man is one of plunder,
        one of avarice,
        one of violence to his fellow man.

The storm of man is one of satanic impulses,
        one of demonic actions,
        one of evil personified on the face of man.

The storm of man sees the butchering of man by the butchery of man,
        sees the blood upon The Earth,
        sees the dismembering of limbs,
        sees the blood-stained shells of man.

The storm of man hears the nights of mourning,
        hears the wailing of the innocent,
        hears the crying of the motherless,
        hears the laughter of the merciless.

The storm of man shouts in victory,
        moans in defeat;
        surges in the onslaught,
        limps in the retreat;
        pockets the gains of looting,
        discards the failed weapons as burdens to the body.

The storm of man signals as it rushes forward,
        signals as it runs away.

The storm of man behaves as if a wave which flows and ebbs.

The storm of man is aware of the thrust and parry at the centre of the conflict—
                      the battle for the prize of man.

    The prize of man is claimed by the blood oaths of the devil,
            by the blood oaths of man,
            by a willing partnership which condemns the
                      participants to the flames of destiny,
            by the perjured partnership where each will blame
                the other for the ignominy of their defeat;
                    for the ignominy of their imprisonment;
                    for the ignominy of their being.

    Beware the storm of man bereft of love,
            of Grace,
            of honour,
            of mercy,

of respect:
towards those who find themselves unwittingly enmeshed within its maul;
as beggars for lives of little worth.

Beware the storm of man as it engulfs a landscape,
as it lays waste a landscape,
as it overruns the defences of inhabitants,
as it generates the piles of charcoal under a blackened sky.

Beware the storm of man which has no quarter,
which has no fear of God,
which has no respite in which to flee,
which has no recompense for bravery,
which has no safe passage for a bribe.

The storm of man is a storm of death built upon destruction.

The storm of man is a storm of evil built upon encouragement.

The storm of man is a storm of greed built upon the plunder.

The storm of man is a storm of self-enrichment built upon the loot.

The storm of man spreads as if catching a fever which rages in the brain,
as if bringing the loss of reason to the senses,
as if caring not for abandoned loved ones,
as if deserted by a memory of values—
no longer deemed as valid.

The storm of man is intensified by the storm of Satan,
is an admixture of the two,
is dependent for its ferocity on agreement—
as the physical blends with the spiritual.

The storm of man is a maelstrom of confusion,
a maelstrom of blood lust,
a maelstrom of discontent,
a maelstrom of anger in release,
a maelstrom of vengeance running wild,
a maelstrom of identity discarded.

The storm of man is the killing spree of the century where evil reigns at the will of man.

The storm of man grieves The Holy Spirit of God."

My Content Study Aid

_____

_____

The Glory of Enthronement

"The reality of the existence of man beyond the grave of his mortality
                             lies within The Faith of man,
                             lies within the mysteries of God,
                             lies within The Will of The Father.

The reality of the onward existence of man should leave little room for doubt in the
                             experience of those who choose to walk with God,
                             of those who choose to be with God,
                             of those who choose to serve their God
                                                     of Love.

The reality of the onward existence of man is a fact confirmed by God,
                         is a promise made by God,
                         is in a sacrifice made by God.

The reality of the onward existence of man has testimonies of the martyrs,
                         has testimonies of the witnesses at a grave,
                         has testimonies arising from the inquisition
                                         of man,
                         has testimonies which stood and stand
                                         without rescinding:
                                         even unto a tortured death.

The reality of the onward existence of man is but a handshake from the supra-natural
                                                                        realm of God.

     The supra-natural realm of God impacts on the natural realm of man at The Will
                                                                   of God.

     The supra-natural realm of God impacts on the natural realm of man
                                         through the presence of My Spirit,
                                         through the gifts of My Spirit,
                                         through the supra-natural abilities vested
                                         in My servants which have extended
                                         testimonies to include the signs,
                                                   the wonders,
                                                   the miracles as brought by
                                                            My Spirit before
                                         all the senses of man,
                                     all the confessors of their Faith.

     The scoffers and the sceptics,
                 with all who know not righteousness,
                 will carry their false beliefs,
                 will carry their deeds as likened to hay or straw,

to be challenged by the fire which tests:
so the truth will accompany them into the godlessness of their
eternity after they appear as summoned to
attend The Great White Throne of God.

The reality of the onward existence of man in the supra-natural realm of God is the
evidence of the miracles,
the wonders,
the signs—
the out workings of My Spirit in the contorted
realm of man where evil holds its sway.

The reality of the onward existence of man carries either the honour of his labours,
or the respect due empty hands.

The reality of the onward existence of man has his senses opened to the reality of the
realm of God.

The reality of the onward existence of man has the evidence of the visitors—
those who have been and returned bearing witness:
of the reality of the realm of God.

The reality of the realm of God should not be in dispute by man,
should not be in doubt as communication proceeds
therewith continuously,
should not be denied unless by the noisy fool who cannot
tell the night from day.

The reality of the realm of God is the final stepping stone of progression in the life
of man,
is the final stepping stone of man where his destiny
remains a freewill choice,
is the final stepping stone of dwelling.

The reality of the realm of God is not a boring place,
is the showplace of the stars of God,
is the origin of creation,
is extensive and devout.

The reality of the realm of God has the garden of Eden with The Tree of Life intact—
The Tree of Life waiting there to welcome His sheep into His Presence,
waiting there to welcome His Kings unto The Glory of enthronement,
waiting there assembled to greet The Family of God.

The Glory of enthronement fails in its description in the languages of man.

The Glory of enthronement is as the sun shining through a cloud of pearls,
is as The Light of rainbows,
is as the curtains of the northern lights,
is as the flickering of fire in the service of man.

The Glory of enthronement attests to the design of God,
                attests to the beauty of creation,
                attests to the choreography of the music master of
                                        the heavens,
                attests to the music and the dancers at one with the chords
                                            of light.

The Glory of enthronement does not cast a shadow,
                does not have an echo,
                does not simulate that upon The Earth.

The Glory of enthronement has the shining of the gold,
                the shining of the silver,
                the shining of the jewels of God where there is no need
                                            to burnish.

The Glory of enthronement has lace work with its intricacy,
                has satin with its sheen,
                has silk of iridescence,
                has brocades of grandeur,
                has the gowns of life glowing with the life inside,
                has the crowns for kings awaiting coronations,
                has the throne of homage in the midst of the throne of Grace
                                            and the throne of fire.

The Glory of enthronement is not a once off spectacle,
                is not dependent on establishing a memory,
                is not subject to photography.

The Glory of enthronement continues with man's spirit in his throne room,
                continues in the absence of time,
                continues without abatement,
                        without refreshment,
                        without renewal of a theme.

The Glory of enthronement is built on the beauty of man in perfection of style and form
                                                      within the realm of God.

The Glory of enthronement sees man in possession of all which was declared in the
                                                    promises of God.
The Glory of enthronement sees man with his inheritance.
The Glory of enthronement sees man as God designed him so to be.

The Glory of enthronement is the ultimate expression of the love of God.
The Glory of enthronement is embedded in the heavens.
The Glory of enthronement is attached to The Will of God.
The Glory of enthronement is the reward for service done with honour as a
                                                              willing servant.

The Glory of enthronement is the result of decorating the gown of life with the decorations which withstood the fire.

The Glory of enthronement shares a relationship with God.

The Glory of enthronement never fades away.

The Glory of enthronement places man upon his pinnacle where the vista is superb, where man can see forever, where man can hold the hand of God.

The Glory of enthronement is the ultimate accolade of God."

My Content Study Aid

_____
_____
_____
_____
_____
_____
_____
_____
_____
_____
_____
_____
_____
_____
_____
_____
_____
_____
_____
_____

Book of Ezekiel— Intent of Divine Commentary

"This day,
>Anthony,
>>I disclose My intent to make known My commentary on
>>>The Book of Ezekiel—
>>>>similar in style and layout as you have received in the days gone by—
>>>>>as for The Book of Revelation,
>>>>>as for The Book of Daniel.

For in these days approaching man will he be in need of understanding,
>will he be in need of wisdom prior to acting,
>will he be left in confusion if he hearkens to the voice of man,
>will he be left in mortal danger if he forgets his covering.

This day,
>Anthony,
>>continues your period of the preparation of My scrolls,
>>>your period of discernment,
>>>your period of listening,
>>>your period of writing as My scribe.

This day,
>Anthony,
>>will My commentary on the writings of Ezekiel be related
>>>in these days and time,
>>>in these technologies and cultures,
>>>in these networks with their reach;
>>for then the values adopted by man may be appraised by man,
>>>may be reviewed by man,
>>>may be modified by man:
>>>may be compared with the values held
>>>>stationary by God."

Received 12.36— 1.11 pm Friday, 16th September 2011
Hamilton, NZ

Scribal Note: *There are no specific divine commentaries on the content of verses within the chapters: 5, 12— 13, 16— 18, 23, 26, 35. Upon enquiry of The Spirit as to the absence of such commentaries on these, The Lord shares His divine intent for each particular chapter at the start of each.*

For completeness and transparency, there are a number of divine revelatory texts previously made known in His first book 'God Speaks of Return and Bannered' *under the heading* **The Divine Scriptural Revelations** *' whose subject is* "banners", "signs" *and* "standards".

These three earlier texts are copied and placed here in this book in the applicable chapters and verses of the 'Divine Commentary' *part of* The Book of Ezekiel *and is noted therein and described:*
'**As in My book**— ':
Ezekiel 20:12, 24:24, 24:27.

The Blue Letter Bible is acknowledged with gratitude for its practical assistance with NKJV Text entry.
www.blueletterbible.org/

Copyright Information, New King James Version, © 1982 by Thomas Nelson, Inc. All rights reserved. Used by permission.

My Content Study Aid

_____
_____
_____
_____
_____
_____
_____
_____
_____
_____
_____
_____
_____
_____
_____
_____
_____
_____
_____
_____

"My message for My souls—
The Living Souls of God"

Divine Commentary— Ezekiel Ch 01

Eze 1:1 Now it came to pass in the thirtieth year, in the fourth *month,* on the fifth *day* of the month, as I *was* among the captives by the River Chebar, *that* the heavens were opened and I saw visions of God.
Divine Commentary—
"The visions seen by Ezekiel have rightly been ascribed to God,
     have rightly been viewed as from God,
     have rightly been perceived as from the throne of God.

The visions seen by Ezekiel were manifest and true,
     were captured and described,
     were inscribed upon a scroll with a destiny of centuries,
          with a destiny of instruction,
          with a destiny of forbearance,
          with a destiny conjoined with
               the ending of the age of Grace.

The visions seen by Ezekiel are of tolerance and discipline,
     are of reason and responsibility,
     are of damage and repair.

The visions seen by Ezekiel suffer punishment for sin,
     suffer the pain drawn down into the present,
     suffer the watchman on the battlements,
          the guard within the watchtower.

The visions seen by Ezekiel speak of the wanderers who know not where to stand,
          who know not how to blow
               a trumpet,
          who know not how to arouse the
               bewildered and befogged."

Eze 1:3 the word of the LORD came expressly to Ezekiel the priest, the son of Buzi, in the land of the Chaldeans by the River Chebar; and the hand of the LORD was upon him there.
Divine Commentary—
"The visions of God are often not recorded by man,
     not recorded as a marker from his God,
     not recorded as a marker within his life,
     not recorded as a marker for his offspring.

The visions of God are often left to fall as a leaf upon The Earth,
     left to fall into a waste bin filled with the approaches
          of God,
     left to fall from where such are never resurrected,

left to fall as clutter without value from a shuttered spirit
with a shuttered soul.

The visions of God should be deemed as turning points in the life of man,
should be validated by the spirit,
should be welcomed by the soul,
should be actioned by the body,
should be written for the record in a time of celebration,
should be borne as testimony of The Living God.

The visions of God should be nurtured to fruition,
should be seen to build line upon line,
should be seen to impart precept upon precept,
should be a part of all which whispers of a calling,
which leads into assuredness,
which confirms the direction of the footsteps in the comfort of The Lord,
which affirms the counsel of My Spirit to the heart of man."

Eze 1:20 Wherever the spirit wanted to go, they went, *because* there the spirit went; and the wheels were lifted together with them, for the spirit of the living creatures *was* in the wheels.
Divine Commentary—

"The vision of Ezekiel has a simile in man,
links understanding of the environment of Heaven to the reality
of man,
speaks wisdom to the spirit of man as comprehension of a vision
brings perception of intent to the mind of man.

The vision of Ezekiel is a transplant designed to flourish,
is the sketching of an artist,
is the visual which imposes difficulties on the vocabularies of man,
is the footprint of Heaven placed beside the footprint of man,
is the proffered hand of God there for the grasp of man,
is the handshake of the heavens awaiting the handshakes of
The Earth."

Eze 1:21 When those went, *these* went; when those stood, *these* stood; and when those were lifted up from The Earth, the wheels were lifted up together with them, for the spirit of the living creatures *was* in the wheels.
Divine Commentary—

"For as the vision of Ezekiel unfolds so the actions become apparent,
so the relevance is seen,
so the purpose is displayed before the eyes and ears
of man as bounded by his spirit.

Oh that man would extend the bounding of his spirit.
Oh that man would set the scene of welcome for The Holy Spirit.

Oh that man would seek The Wisdom of God—
>> the harbinger of knowledge,
>> replete with understanding,
>> in this age of Grace."

Eze 1:22 The likeness of the firmament above the heads of the living creatures *was* like the colour of an awesome crystal, stretched out over their heads.
Divine Commentary—

"So the vision of Ezekiel includes aspects of The Earth with aspects of the heavens,
> includes translation to The Earth,
> includes transition to the heavens.

So the vision of Ezekiel brings consideration of the divine into the consideration of man,
> brings The Glory of a kingdom into one about to be,
> brings the foreshadowing of expectation into the reality of man.

So the vision of Ezekiel carries clarity of detail,
> carries fullness of expression,
> carries that which lingers until the closure of the age of Grace,
> carries in Faith and substance the intended message as sent from God to man."

Eze 1:23 And under the firmament their wings *spread out* straight, one toward another. Each one had two which covered one side, and each one had two which covered the other side of the body.
Divine Commentary—

"So the wings of might change their orientation,
> change their spatial relationships,
> change to conform to the environment wherein they are,
> change to reflect the image of the moment,
> change to enhance the honouring of the circumstance,
> change to portray The Holiness of being,
> change to satisfy the compliance due to Heaven."

Eze 1:24 When they went, I heard the noise of their wings, like the noise of many waters, like the voice of the Almighty, a tumult like the noise of an army; and when they stood still, they let down their wings.
Divine Commentary—

"So the positioning of the wings,
  the actions of the wings,
  the posture of the wings are of exceeding importance within the vision of Ezekiel.

So the noise of the wings is emphasized,
 so the sound of the wings is compared,
 so the folding of the wings is noted at their standing still,
 so the wings convey their meanings within the vision of Ezekiel."

Eze 1:25 A voice came from above the firmament that *was* over their heads; whenever they stood, they let down their wings.
Divine Commentary—

"The voice of God can speak into a vision,
        can speak into a dream,
        can speak into the written word,
        can speak into the scripture,
        can speak into the mind of man,
        can speak into the ear of man.

The voice of God can speak into the lifelines of two-way communication,
        can speak into the reception of the sixth sense of man,
        can welcome a transmission from the sixth sense of man.

The voice of God can speak without occurrence of delay of distance,
        can speak in response faster than The Light is emitted from the sun,
        can speak across the cosmos without attenuation.

The voice of God is everywhere abounding,
        is heard with clarity of diction,
        is not in need of man's translation,
        is neither subject to a fade nor wane,
        is without impediment to understanding,
        is transmitted by My Spirit in accordance with My message."

Eze 1:26 And above the firmament over their heads *was* the likeness of a throne, in appearance like a sapphire stone; on the likeness of the throne *was* a likeness with the appearance of a man high above it.
Divine Commentary—

"The vision of Ezekiel continues unabated,
        continues as he lifts his eyes,
        continues with what his eyes beheld."

Eze 1:27 Also from the appearance of His waist and upward I saw, as it were, the colour of amber with the appearance of fire all around within it; and from the appearance of His waist and downward I saw, as it were, the appearance of fire with brightness all around.
Divine Commentary—

"The vision of Ezekiel continues with his description of a figure garbed above the waist:
        with the appearance of amber-coloured fire as if contained within;
            while also garbed upon his lower half:
        with the appearance of fire whereon fell surrounding brightness."

Eze 1:28 Like the appearance of a rainbow in a cloud on a rainy day, so *was* the appearance of the brightness all around it. This *was* the appearance of the likeness of the glory of the LORD. So when I saw *it,* I fell on my face, and I heard a voice of One speaking.
Divine Commentary—

"The vision of Ezekiel has a meaning for these days of fulfilment;
 for as Grace draws to a close,
 for as The Bride minds her white linen:
   so this vision of Ezekiel has significance.

This,
 My commentary,
 is for The End-time understanding of man.

As Ezekiel looks he beholds a whirlwind of fire,
  a boiling cauldron of fire feeding on itself,
   engulfing whilst expanding,
  raging within a cloud radiating brightness from its midst:
   a transparent envelope with an amber colour arising from the
    centre of the fireball.

The four sentinels of God emanate from within the fireball in the image of the likeness of
    a man:
  to stand the test of time until a mystery of God reaches its set time
    for disclosure.

Each sentinel has four faces,
 each sentinel has four wings,
 each sentinel is a semblance of four living creatures—
   the guardians of the throne room of God.

Their legs are straight—
 are not the cause of deviations.

The soles of their feet are fresh and still tender—
   like those of calves—
   for bringing 'Good News' unto the mountains:
    the high places,
    the pinnacles,
    the citadels—
   where false claims to sovereignty are often not disturbed.

The soles of their feet are clean and glisten,
  are polished to a shine in preparation for development:
    so 'You who bring good tidings,
    Get up into the high mountain;
    O Jerusalem,
     You who bring good tidings,
     Lift up your voice with strength,
     Lift it up,
      be not afraid;
     Say to the cities of Judah,
      "Behold your God!" '*

So each face is endowed with two hands of a man enclosed on each side under
their wings;
are under the authority of a man and the authority of The Holy Spirit:
the bearers of the two sets of wings.

Their wings are in accord,
touch to signify the unity in the counselling by The Holy Spirit of the spirit of
a man.

They do not vary from a direct line in their travels forward.

Each of their four faces are likened to those within the experience of man.

To the front of each is the face of an eagle—
at the front to lead with the power and authority of The Holy Spirit which goes before to
guide and to counsel:
My Spirit as now known to man,
He who is The Comforter,
He who prepares the way,
He who brings counselling as to The Will of God,
He who sheds light into the darkness:
unto the feet of man.

To the right side of each is the face of a lion:
The Lion of Judah,
The Lord Jesus,
The Messiah,
the elder brother of a man—
the senior member of a relationship:
as a man becomes adopted into The Family of God.

To the left side of each is the face of an ox—
with the strength,
the might,
the presence of The Father:
with The Wisdom and authority
to oversee an act of love,
to oversee an act of sacrifice,
to oversee an act of forgiveness,
to oversee an act of judgment in The Kingdom of His Son,
in the presence of a man.

So attention is drawn to the semblance of a man being in the loving presence,
being in the bounding presence,
of the semblances of The Trinity of God.

To the rear is the face of a man:
that his semblance may move,
in Faith and by his testimony,

    as he follows the leading of My Spirit.

Their wings stretch upwards as they point to a destination.

Their two upper wings are those of an eagle—
    a semblance of The Holy Spirit with the word of The Lord.

    These two wings are—
    The Truth of the counsel of My Spirit and The Purity of The Bride of Christ.

The two lower wings are those of a man—
    his Faith and his Testimony:
    the two which cover their bodies in semblance of
        their likeness.

When they stand they let down their wings in reverence,
 when they are under the firmament their wings spread out straight in acknowledgment.

The strength of the wings determines the temporary assignment of surroundings.

Each sentinel has freedom of movement—
    accompanies the spirit of man wherever the spirit chooses to go:
    never leaves the spirit,
      always moves in straight lines maintaining righteousness—
      does not deviate,
      does not bend,
      does not compromise the straightness of direction,
    which confirms and leads,
    to the destination.

Their appearance is like burning coals of fire,
    like incandescent flames,
    like fiery embers with full ignition,
    like the glowing basis of a furnace,
    like the Holy Fire of God.

For both My Spirit and the spirit of a man accompany each sentinel,
    each spirit can carry a flaming torch fed from the fire of Heaven:
    the fire of My Spirit's torch which ignites the torch of the spirit of
        a man.

So the torches ascribed to each sentinel are seen going back and forth,
    are seen going to and fro,
      as if searchlights in among the sentinels,
      as they traverse their surroundings.

The fire in its brightness is laced with offshoots of lightning—
      as if despatched as arrows from a bow.

As they run back and forth so the living creatures appear to be like a flash of lightning—
      like a flash from an arrow tipped with fire:

with but a short time of existence.

Then Ezekiel sees a wheel on The Earth beside each sentinel with its four faces.

All four wheels,
> with their workings,
> appear a transparent pale blue,
> while also being of the same likeness.

All four of their workings are,
> as they so appear to be,
> each existing as a wheel in the middle of a wheel.

My Spirit is in harmony,
> in unison,
> with the spirit of a man:
> a wheel within a wheel,
> both meshing with the other in unity of purpose:
> wherein My Spirit is closely aligned with the spirit of a man.

My Spirit is with a man—
> in close contact with the spirit of a man.

When the wheels move,
> they go towards any one of four directions,
> do not deviate from their path of choice:
>> from their highway of intent—
>> from their direction of travel.

The wheels stop at the way stations of The Lord,
> at the turning points of life,
> at a call for a change in direction,
> at a visit for inspection.

My Spirit and the spirit of a man make use of the eyes of a man,
> see everything he sees,
> can see as if located on enormous bounding rims:
>> the peripheries,
>> the perimeters,
> can see through all the degrees found within a
>> turning circle,
>> as the body moves its head,
>> as the body rotates,
>> as the eyes look up and down.

When the sentinels of God go,
> the wheels go beside them.

When the sentinels of God stand,
> the wheels stand.

When the sentinels are lifted up from The Earth,
> the wheels are lifted up.

So it is The Spirit of the Living God accompanies the spirit of a man:
> as a man exercises his freewill when on The Earth.

So it is The Spirit of the Living God still accompanies the spirit of a man when the
> sentinels of his body are lifted up from The Earth,
>> are lifted up from the grave of a man,
>> are lifted up towards the firmament,
>>> above which is a likeness of a throne.

On the likeness of a throne is a likeness with the appearance of a man high above it.

So Ezekiel's eyes beheld that which he has recorded,
> as being within the appearance of bright fire,
> as being like a rainbow in a cloud on a rainy day giving
>> the appearance of brightness all around:
>> of the likeness of The Glory of The Lord.

The vision of Ezekiel speaks of where a body goes and why;
> of how a body goes and when.

The vision of Ezekiel speaks into this age of Grace,
> speaks into the immortality of a man as he rises unto judgment,
>> as he rises unto blessings,
>> as he rises from the grave."

Scribal Note: *Scripture reference for that as selected by The Lord for insertion here—* Isaiah 40:9 NKJV

> "… O Zion,
> You who bring good tidings,
> Get up into the high mountain;
> O Jerusalem,
> You who bring good tidings,
> Lift up your voice with strength,
> Lift it up, be not afraid;
> Say to the cities of Judah, "Behold your God!"

My Content Study Aid

_____
_____
_____
_____

Divine Commentary— Ezekiel Ch 02

Eze 2:1 And He said to me, "Son of man, stand on your feet, and I will speak to you."
Divine Commentary—

"I,
    The Lord,
        speak to those to whom I will:
                to those who know of preparation,
                to those who know to listen,
                to those who know their Faith,
                to those who know to answer,
                to those who know My wisdom,
                to those who know The Fear of The Lord."

Eze 2:2 Then the Spirit entered me when He spoke to me, and set me on my feet; and I heard Him who spoke to me.
Divine Commentary—

"In the days of Ezekiel did My Spirit enter.

In the age of Grace is My Spirit present,
        is My Spirit active throughout the life of discipleship,
        is My Spirit willing to converse with the spirit of man."

Eze 2:3 And He said to me: "Son of man, I am sending you to the children of Israel, to a rebellious nation that has rebelled against Me; they and their fathers have transgressed against Me to this very day.
Divine Commentary—

"As I,
    The Lord,
        speak to My Prophets:
                so I expect to be obeyed,
                so I expect My message to go forth,
                so I expect reactions of sincerity,
                so I expect attitudes to change,
                so I expect lives to be affected,
                so I expect nations to embrace the morality declared,
                so I expect man to be prepared,
                so I expect My Bride to be ready for Her Groom."

Eze 2:4 "For *they are* impudent and stubborn children. I am sending you to them, and you shall say to them, 'Thus says The Lord GOD.'
Divine Commentary—

"For as My message is also to the stubborn so it may have to be repeated,
                        so it may have to be re-emphasized,

                    so it may have to be delivered with clarity
                            of insight:

    devoid of interference from another source;
    devoid of a reason,
        without a basis of validity,
            which is inserted between the message and reception;
    devoid of an intrusion preventing comprehension of that which is expected;
    devoid of any matter which will impact on rejection,
        other than as decided by the heart,
            within the freewill of man."

Eze 2:5 "As for them, whether they hear or whether they refuse—for they *are* a rebellious house—yet they will know that a prophet has been among them.
Divine Commentary—

"For whether or not they incline their ears to hear in the midst of their rebellion,
    yet will they recall the day a prophet comes among them,
        the day they stamp their feet,
            the day his voice is heard with a message from their God."

Eze 2:6 "And you, son of man, do not be afraid of them nor be afraid of their words, though briers and thorns *are* with you and you dwell among scorpions; do not be afraid of their words or dismayed by their looks, though they *are* a rebellious house.
Divine Commentary—

"For as My prophet goes,
    so My prophet carries.

For as My prophet is hindered,
    so My prophet overcomes.

For as My prophet is nervous,
    so My prophet is strengthened.

For as My prophet encounters the confrontations of man,
    so My prophet will know The Wisdom of My Spirit."

Eze 2:7 "You shall speak My words to them, whether they hear or whether they refuse, for they *are* rebellious.
Divine Commentary—

"The prophet speaks under the auspices of God,
    speaks whether into acceptance or rejection,
    speaks whether into agreement or rebellion."

Eze 2:8 "But you, son of man, hear what I say to you. Do not be rebellious like that rebellious house; open your mouth and eat what I give you."
Divine Commentary—

"But you,
    O prophet in your mortality,

> value My words to you,
>> place them close to your heart;
>>> thereby protecting yourself from catching the disease of those to whom you are sent."

Eze 2:9 Now when I looked, there was a hand stretched out to me; and behold, a scroll of a book *was* in it.
Divine Commentary—

> "Now as the prophet looks,
>> there is a hand stretched out to him;
>>> and behold,
>>>> a scroll of a book is in it,
>>>> a scroll of a vision is in it,
>>>> a scroll of The End-time age of Grace is in it:
>>> a scroll of preparation for The Bride,
>>> a scroll of the harvest in these awaited days of rain,
>>> a scroll of the coming storm prior to the clouds of conquest."

Scribal Note:

On Servants and Divine Intent:

From Chapter 3 onwards all further Divine Commentaries relate to Servants in their Servanthood. These form a grand exposition of the qualities found in 'My' servants (of God) and the counselling of The Holy Spirit of 'My' servants when in service to their God. The behaviour in service of the 3 types of servants is detailed as they follow their figurehead of choice for 'My' servants; 'His' servants; and 'The' servants. They are listed below for easy access and are annotated as such in the Indexes.
Refer:

'My' servants Ch 03— Ch 41, Ch 44— Ch 48

'His' servants Ch 42

'His' and 'My' servants are contrasted in Ch 43

'The' servants of The Earth in Ch 43

Each of these 9 chapters have a Divine Intent but no Divine Commentaries—
05, 12-13, 16-18, 23, 26, 35.

There is a Divine Intent at the beginning of each chapter— of these, the latter six refer to Jerusalem (4), to Israel (3), to Samaria (1), to Palestine (1), to Tyre (1), and to Mount Seir (1): in an intertwining of relationships.

Ch 05	Ch 12	Ch 13
Ch 16	Ch 17	Ch 18
Ch 23	Ch 26	Ch 35

Divine Commentary— Ezekiel Ch 03

Eze 3:1 Moreover He said to me, "Son of man, eat what you find; eat this scroll, and go, speak to the house of Israel."
Divine Commentary—

"My servants do not let their food drop upon The Earth,
        do not let that sent to nourish them lie upon a wasteland,
        do not permit the sacred to become burdened by the secular.

My servants should have an appetite for sacred fare,
        should have a thirst to share the living water,
        should have an urgency to be with all they have been tasked.

My servants do not revoke the root of proclamation,
            the basis of a testimony,
            the sharing of their Faith."

Eze 3:2 So I opened my mouth, and He caused me to eat that scroll.
Divine Commentary—

"My servants serve the word of God.

My servants have the highest calling available to man.

My servants are not prone to faint,
        are not prone to weariness,
        are not prone to change their coat in the middle of My river."

Eze 3:3 And He said to me, "Son of man, feed your belly, and fill your stomach with this scroll that I give you." So I ate, and it was in my mouth like honey in sweetness.
Divine Commentary—

"My servants feast on the fare of God.

My servants are nurtured on the fare of God.

My servants are commissioned with the fare of God laid for the fare of man.

My servants are empowered to partition the fare of God into the sips of man.

My servants are called to invoke the presence of Heaven into the heart of man.

My servants keep an eye single to The Glory of God.

My servants bring great honour within The Fear of God."

Eze 3:4 Then He said to me: "Son of man, go to the house of Israel and speak with My words to them.
Divine Commentary—

"My servants grow and develop,
        are not static in position,

        are not unstable in their outlook.

My servants are fed and watered.
My servants are clothed and sheltered.
My servants are blessed and tended.

My servants are not left alone,
        are never deserted as on an island,
        are never caught up with no escape.

My servants are under the close scrutiny of God,
        are under the fire of My Spirit,
        are under the commander of the angels,
        are under the throne of God with the cherubim at large,
        are under the mantle covering attached to every calling,
        are under the oversight of an open Heaven,
        are under the counsel of My Spirit guiding within The Will of God."

Eze 3:20 "Again, when a righteous *man* turns from his righteousness and commits iniquity, and I lay a stumbling block before him, he shall die; because you did not give him warning, he shall die in his sin, and his righteousness which he has done shall not be remembered; but his blood I will require at your hand.
Divine Commentary—

"My servants carry accountability for their ministry in My name,
        carry accountability for the accuracy of a message purported as divine,
        carry accountability for a tongue of rampant volubility.

My servants carry accountability for all remarks which issue when before a sacred
                                    position of authority.

My servants uphold the sanctity of callings,
        the sanctity of The Edifice of God,
        the sanctity of the empowering of God."

Eze 3:21 "Nevertheless if you warn the righteous *man* that the righteous should not sin, and he does not sin, he shall surely live because he took warning; also you will have delivered your soul."
Divine Commentary—

"My servants deliver the accurate messages of God with the impunity granted to
                                    His messengers,
                        with impunity from culpability,
                        with impunity from recompense,
                        with impunity from implication.

My servants need not forestall the sin implicit in a message,
        need not reiterate a message once delivered,
        need not emphasize a segment in delivery of a message.

My servants should not append their interpretation to the vocabulary of God."

Eze 3:22 Then the hand of the LORD was upon me there, and He said to me, "Arise, go out into the plain, and there I shall talk with you."
Divine Commentary—

"My servants need to have two-way communication,
>need a relationship of honour,
>need a time of Holiness before the throne of God.

My servants should know The Will of God,
>should know The Wisdom of God,
>should seek and they will find.

My servants are empowered to ask,
>are empowered to expect an open window,
>are empowered to offer praise,
>are empowered to worship at an altar to The Living God:
>>whether in the wilderness of man or in a sanctuary of God.

My servants are commissioned to impart their knowledge of the ways of God,
>to impart their knowledge of the giftings of My Spirit,
>to instigate the quest for the baptism of My Spirit,
>to instigate the seeking of the reality of The Loving God
>>by His children—
>by His children in ignorance of what is held in store
>>for those at large outside the fold of God;
>>for those at ease within the fold of God."

My Content Study Aid

_____
_____
_____
_____
_____
_____
_____
_____
_____
_____
_____

Divine Commentary— Ezekiel Ch 04

Eze 4:1 "You also, son of man, take a clay tablet and lay it before you, and portray on it a city, Jerusalem.
Divine Commentary—
"My servants are expected to follow the counsel of My Spirit,
        are expected to use The Wisdom of The Lord in their walk with man,
        are expected to not defer that set for the attention of this day."

Eze 4:2 "Lay siege against it, build a siege wall against it, and heap up a mound against it; set camps against it also, and place battering rams against it all around.
Divine Commentary—
"My servants when they listen are in receipt of detailed directions that point to
                                            ultimate success,
        are in receipt of the attention of their God,
        are in receipt of wisdom unavailable from man.

My servants should hearken to receive—
        expecting to receive—
        waiting to receive—
        their directions for the day.

My servants are to attend with excellence to the fore,
        are not to linger in a lane which winds and twists,
        are not to sleep under a hedge of briars.

My servants may sleep under a tree of oak,
        under a tree of strength,
        under a tree which shelters from a storm."

Eze 4:3 "Moreover take for yourself an iron plate, and set it *as* an iron wall between you and the city. Set your face against it, and it shall be besieged, and you shall lay siege against it. This *will be* a sign to the house of Israel.
Divine Commentary—
"My servants should know the storm from which they shelter,
        should know its makeup and its content,
        should know its purpose and its reach,
        should know its objective and its weapons,
        should know the place of danger,
        should know the place of safety,
        should know the encampment of The Lord."

Eze 4:4 "Lie also on your left side, and lay the iniquity of the house of Israel upon it. *According* to the number of the days that you lie on it, you shall bear their iniquity.
Divine Commentary—

"For I would that My servants should seek and find to dwell in the encampment of
The Lord when a storm befalls,
when a storm invades,
when a storm despatches,
when a storm threatens,
when a storm brings the roar of desolation,
brings the roar of inundation,
brings the roar which impedes the service of My servants."

My Content Study Aid

Divine Intent— Ezekiel Ch 05

Scribal Note: *There are no specific divine commentaries on the content verses within this chapter.*

Upon enquiry of The Spirit as to the absence of such commentaries on Ezekiel Ch 05, The Lord shares His divine intent on this chapter:

"The query of the fool and the query of the wise sometimes overlap,
    sometimes seek an answer to what is already laid before them,
        sometimes do not recall the relevance of a rebuke from the past in applying to
            the conditions in the making—
                in the end-times of this age of Grace."

My Content Study Aid

Divine Commentary— Ezekiel Ch 06

Eze 6:1 Now the word of the LORD came to me, saying:
Divine Commentary—
"My servants acknowledge what I say,
>   listen to what I say,
>   remember what I say."

Eze 6:2 "Son of man, set your face toward the mountains of Israel, and prophesy against them,
Divine Commentary—
"My servants follow in the way of what they are asked,
>   follow with promptness to perform,
>   follow to announce the text as it is received."

Eze 6:3 "and say, 'O mountains of Israel, hear the word of the Lord GOD! Thus says the Lord GOD to the mountains, to the hills, to the ravines, and to the valleys: "Indeed I, *even* I, will bring a sword against you, and I will destroy your high places.
Divine Commentary—
"So My servants address My word to the intended,
>   address the subject with great care,
>   address the content with sincere deliberation."

Eze 6:4 "Then your altars shall be desolate, your incense altars shall be broken, and I will cast down your slain *men* before your idols.
Divine Commentary—
"So My servants deliver the message within the context,
>   the content with clarity of expression,
>   the circumstance of penalties of disobedience which may change
>   rebuke to wrath."

Eze 6:5 "And I will lay the corpses of the children of Israel before their idols, and I will scatter your bones all around your altars.
Divine Commentary—
"So My servants should be prepared for what they may be asked to announce,
>   to utter as an edict,
>   to pronounce the passion
>   of God to fall upon the wayward,
>   upon the rebellious,
>   upon those grounded in idolatry:
>   as each is seen to suffer the wages due his sin."

Eze 6:6 "In all your dwelling places the cities shall be laid waste, and the high places shall be desolate, so that your altars may be laid waste and made desolate, your idols may

be broken and made to cease, your incense altars may be cut down, and your works may be abolished.
Divine Commentary—

"So My servants should know the extent of the desolation which may befall man
        in his surroundings,
   the extent of the destruction laying waste his dwellings,
   the extent to which there is a remnant left surviving."

Eze 6:14 'So I will stretch out My hand against them and make the land desolate, yes, more desolate than the wilderness toward Diblah, in all their dwelling places. Then they shall know that I *am* the LORD.' " ' "
Divine Commentary—

"For My servants should beware of such as those who quell life within its sanctuary,
   should beware of such as those who bring unremitting violence,
   should beware of such as those who blaspheme with their lips all which
        God declares as sacred."

My Content Study Aid

Divine Commentary— Ezekiel Ch 07

Eze 7:1   Moreover the word of the LORD came to me, saying,
Divine Commentary—

"When I,
> The Lord,
>> speak to My servants so their attention is sought,
>>> so their abilities are sought,
>>> so their mantle is sought
>>>> in order to exercise The Will of God,
>>>> in order to progress The Will of God,
>>>> in order to establish The Will of God before
>>>>> the face of man.

The will of God is not a document bound and layered in a safe,
> is not a deposit in a closet which rarely sees The Light,
> is not a fractured beam of light emitted without a focus.

The will of God upholds the goal set for all the cultures on The Earth,
> upholds the variance of comprehension set for every culture on
>> The Earth,
> upholds the message of salvation for assimilation by each culture on
>> The Earth.

The will of God is constant in intent,
> is constant in application,
> is constant in its rendering to man.

The will of God is bound by the freewill gift to man,
> initiated the freewill gift to man,
> knows all the implications of the freewill gift to man.

The will of God honours or respects the freewill gift to man.

The will of God embraces all aspects of the freewill gift to man,
> prepares the welcome mat,
> prepares the chains of choice.

The will of God encircles and regards,
> counsels and encourages,
> rewards and tempers judgment.

The will of God is everywhere abounding,
> is known by the discerning,
> is hidden from satanic interference.

The will of God is immune to attack,

> is immune to deception,
> is immune to corruption,
> is immune to all that carries sin.

The will of God listens to the righteous,
> listens to the widows,
> listens to the orphans,
> listens to the humble and the poor.

The will of God listens to all within the offer of His Grace.

The will of God is the glue of families,
> is the glue of love,
> is the glue which binds into eternity with God.

The will of God is the highest court for the appeal of man,
> oversees decisions made with access to the truth,
> translates the intent of the heart of man into the jurisdiction
>> of his choice.

The will of God is the constructor of the records of man,
> is the constructor of the being of man,
> is the constructor of his spirit and his soul.

The will of God erases and forecloses on the life of man.
The will of God extends and multiplies the life of man.
The will of God is implicit in the life of man."

My Content Study Aid

_____
_____
_____
_____
_____
_____
_____
_____
_____
_____
_____
_____

Divine Commentary— Ezekiel Ch 08

Eze 8:1 And it came to pass in the sixth year, in the sixth *month,* on the fifth *day* of the month, as I sat in my house with the elders of Judah sitting before me, that the hand of the Lord GOD fell upon me there.
Divine Commentary—

"So I,
    The Lord,
        speak to My servants in a time of significance,
            in a time of far-reaching change,
            in a time requiring preparation for the storm:
                the storm with many faces which will destroy
                      the livelihoods of man."

Eze 8:2 Then I looked, and there was a likeness, like the appearance of fire—from the appearance of His waist and downward, fire; and from His waist and upward, like the appearance of brightness, like the colour of amber.
Divine Commentary—

"For in the might of God are the people reminded of their sin,
        are the people convicted of their sin,
        are the people found within the presence of their idols."

Eze 8:3 He stretched out the form of a hand, and took me by a lock of my hair; and the Spirit lifted me up between earth and heaven, and brought me in visions of God to Jerusalem, to the door of the north gate of the inner *court,* where the seat of the image of jealousy *was,* which provokes to jealousy.
Divine Commentary—

"For in the authority of God are My servants directed to observe,
        are My servants brought to see,
        are My servants led to witness the dreadful iniquities:
            as practised in the foul dankness of the dark and locked,
            as practised under oath,
            as practised under blood,
            as practised outside The Fear of God,
            as practised within the cravings of the world."

Eze 8:4 And behold, the glory of the God of Israel *was* there, like the vision that I saw in the plain.
Divine Commentary—

"For in the majesty of God is My Glory beheld."

Eze 8:5 Then He said to me, "Son of man, lift your eyes now toward the north." So I lifted my eyes toward the north, and there, north of the altar gate, was this image of jealousy in the entrance.

Divine Commentary—

"For in The Will of God do My servants see as I intend,
> do they do as I require,
> do they report as I initiate."

Eze 8:12 Then He said to me, "Son of man, have you seen what the elders of the house of Israel do in the dark, every man in the room of his idols? For they say, 'The LORD does not see us, the LORD has forsaken the land.' "
Divine Commentary—

"So My servants are informed of all laid as visions before their eyes:
> of that which is said and done."

Eze 8:13 And He said to me, "Turn again, *and* you will see greater abominations that they are doing."
Divine Commentary—

"Then My servants turn to observe even greater repulsive actions among My people."

Eze 8:14 So He brought me to the door of the north gate of the LORD's house; and to my dismay, women were sitting there weeping for Tammuz.
Divine Commentary—

"Again My servants are shown,
> to their great dismay,
>> women crying over their lost games of chance,
>>> over the wealth of the morrow squandered before the end of day,
>>> over their offerings to idols which take and do not restore."

Eze 8:15 Then He said to me, "Have you seen *this,* O son of man? Turn again, you will see greater abominations than these."
Divine Commentary—

"Then I inquire of My servants if they have ever seen such incredulous behaviour?
I,
> The Lord,
>> say to My servants that they but need to turn again:
>>> to see the full repulsiveness of man acting in flagrant opposition to his God.

>> So I will act.
>> So I will be deaf to their cries.
>> So I will unleash the fury of the storm."

My Content Study Aid

Divine Commentary— Ezekiel Ch 09

Eze 9:1 Then He called out in my hearing with a loud voice, saying, "Let those who have charge over the city draw near, each *with* a deadly weapon in his hand."
Divine Commentary—

"My servants do not carry weapons which will harm the flesh of man,
  do not carry weapons which will impact on the bones of man,
  do not carry weapons which will take away the breath of man,
  do not carry weapons which will be the cause of pain to man,
  do not carry weapons which will bring harm from a distance to man,
  do not carry weapons which will nullify the senses of man."

Eze 9:2 And suddenly six men came from the direction of the upper gate, which faces north, each with his battle-ax in his hand. One man among them *was* clothed with linen and had a writer's inkhorn at his side. They went in and stood beside the bronze altar.
Divine Commentary—

"My servants do not fret at what My angels do,
  do not fret when under the instruction of My Spirit,
  do not fret at the tasking of The Lord."

Eze 9:3 Now the glory of the God of Israel had gone up from the cherub, where it had been, to the threshold of the temple. And He called to the man clothed with linen, who *had* the writer's inkhorn at his side;
Divine Commentary—

"My servants bring to completion their tasks in righteousness,
  bring to completion their tasks as they are set,
  bring to completion their tasks as they are woven in their lives."

Eze 9:4 and the LORD said to him, "Go through the midst of the city, through the midst of Jerusalem, and put a mark on the foreheads of the men who sigh and cry over all the abominations that are done within it."
Divine Commentary—

"My servants no longer serve if righteousness is lost,
  if sin encroaches across a frontier,
  if pride installs a grain of sand which festers."

Eze 9:5 To the others He said in my hearing, "Go after him through the city and kill; do not let your eye spare, nor have any pity.
Divine Commentary—

"My servants know the consequence of sin,
  know the consequence of freewill in the grip of carnality run amok,
  know the consequence for a soul bathed in immorality."

Eze 9:6 "Utterly slay old *and* young men, maidens and little children and women; but

do not come near anyone on whom *is* the mark; and begin at My sanctuary." So they began with the elders who *were* before the temple.
Divine Commentary—

"My servants know the mark of My Spirit,
    know the utterance which satisfies a test,
    know the truth when the evidence is on display,
        is laid upon a table:
           as fruit for inspection,
        is carried as the gifts:
           bestowed when they were sought."

Eze 9:7 Then He said to them, "Defile the temple, and fill the courts with the slain. Go out!" And they went out and killed in the city.
Divine Commentary—

"My servants know of a weapon which they carry,
    which stabs right to the heart yet does no damage,
    which convicts to tears yet does not pain the body,
    which circumcises blackness in all the chambers of a
      heart yet then welcomes the flooding of The Light."

Eze 9:8 So it was, that while they were killing them, I was left *alone;* and I fell on my face and cried out, and said, "Ah, Lord GOD! Will You destroy all the remnant of Israel in pouring out Your fury on Jerusalem?"
Divine Commentary—

"My servants do not fear the drafting of The Lord,
  do not fear as the wheat among the tares,
  do not fear as the sheep among the goats.

My servants are elevated above the flood tide of irreverence which inundates
                the self-confessed:
    who know not the despair attached to that which they bear witness:
      both through their deeds and through their folly."

Eze 9:9 Then He said to me, "The iniquity of the house of Israel and Judah *is* exceedingly great, and the land is full of bloodshed, and the city full of perversity; for they say, 'The LORD has forsaken the land, and the LORD does not see!'
Divine Commentary—

"My servants hear the voice of caring reassurance.

My servants also hear the shouts of bloodlust.

My servants also hear the cries of perversity.

My servants hear the accusations of indifference levelled at their God."

Eze 9:10 "And as for Me also, My eye will neither spare, nor will I have pity, *but* I will recompense their deeds on their own head."
Divine Commentary—

"So the servants of The Lord hear of the end results of sin,
        as each deed is allotted as arisen,
                is allotted without mercy,
                is allotted without exception,
                is allotted each to its own head,
                is allotted when Grace is not invoked,
                is allotted to the detriment of man."

My Content Study Aid

Divine Commentary— Ezekiel Ch 10

Eze 10:1   And I looked, and there in the firmament that was above the head of the cherubim, there appeared something like a sapphire stone, having the appearance of the likeness of a throne.
Divine Commentary—

"My servant looks into the highest Heaven and sees as it is intended
>> for the vision to so yield,
>> for the vision to so confirm,
>> for the vision to so portray before the face of man."

Eze 10:2   Then He spoke to the man clothed with linen, and said, "Go in among the wheels, under the cherub, fill your hands with coals of fire from among the cherubim, and scatter *them* over the city." And he went in as I watched.
Divine Commentary—

"So the vision of righteousness moves among the spirits of man and the semblances
>> of The Spirit of God,
> as a semblance of a righteous servant—
> so enabled to pluck the fire of The Holy Spirit,
>> as coals within His hands,
>> from the midst of the Sentinels:
>> to so scatter as directed."

Eze 10:3   Now the cherubim were standing on the south side of the temple when the man went in, and the cloud filled the inner court.
Divine Commentary—

"My servants are aware of the signs of My Spirit moving in the affairs of man.

My servants await,
> in expectation,
>> the confirming presence of My Spirit's signs when in the venue of
>>> man's surroundings.

My servants come and go with foresight and with wisdom bounded knowledge—
> in the presence of My Spirit's call to move with Grace,
>> with healing,
>> with the gifts to be apportioned to
>>> the watchful and the wise."

My Content Study Aid

Divine Commentary— Ezekiel Ch 11

Eze 11:1 Then the Spirit lifted me up and brought me to the East Gate of the LORD's house, which faces eastward; and there at the door of the gate were twenty-five men, among whom I saw Jaazaniah the son of Azzur, and Pelatiah the son of Benaiah, princes of the people.
Divine Commentary—
"So My servants are transported within a vision which they may encounter:
>as the set time so requires;
>as the set season so discloses;
>as the coming age so demands;
>as the closing age so secures;
>as the activities of My Spirit
>>are so ascribed to
>>The Will of God."

My Content Study Aid

Divine Intent— Ezekiel Ch 12

Scribal Note: *There are no specific divine commentaries on the content verses within this chapter.*

Upon enquiry of The Spirit as to the absence of such commentaries on Ezekiel Ch 12, The Lord shares His divine intent on this chapter:

"Here,
  I,
    The Lord,
        speak to My prophet Ezekiel as an example of how I speak to My prophets
            in the end-times of this age of Grace and trial:
              in the time of the preparation of My Bride,
              in the time of preparation for My return."

My Content Study Aid

Divine Intent— Ezekiel Ch 13

Scribal Note*: There are no specific divine commentaries on the content verses within this chapter.*

Upon enquiry of The Spirit as to the absence of such commentaries on Ezekiel Ch 13, The Lord shares His divine intent on this chapter:

"Here,
  I,
    The Lord,
      speak to My prophet Ezekiel with the word of The Lord valid even
        unto these days with renewed intensity,
        unto these days with the breeding of false prophets,
        unto these days with the outpouring of the lies of the lost,
        unto these days with the women dwelling behind the veils,
        unto these days with the divination of the magic of the stars."

My Content Study Aid

_____
_____
_____
_____
_____
_____
_____
_____
_____
_____
_____
_____
_____
_____
_____
_____
_____
_____
_____
_____

Divine Commentary— Ezekiel Ch 14

Eze 14:1 Now some of the elders of Israel came to me and sat before me.
Divine Commentary—

"So those who should be worthy of esteem as My servants
>> sometimes seek words of exoneration from My prophets—
>>> in consolation of the idolatry of those servants who profane in secrecy."

Eze 14:2 And the word of the LORD came to me, saying,
Divine Commentary—

"So My servants,
> the prophets,
>> are not to grant the desires of these servants,
>> are to say that which their idols have earnt them,
>>> that which they will come to dread,
>>> that which will bring them an audience directed by
>>>> The Lord God."

My Content Study Aid

_____
_____
_____
_____
_____
_____
_____
_____
_____
_____
_____
_____
_____
_____
_____
_____
_____
_____

Divine Commentary— Ezekiel Ch 15

Eze 15:1 Then the word of the LORD came to me, saying:
Divine Commentary—

"My servants become accustomed to the counsel of My Spirit,
    become accustomed to the delivery of the mail,
    become accustomed to the wrapping with the presentation.

My servants do not seek growth within their spirits,
    do not explore the airmail of delivery,
    do not explore courier delivery which has no need of translation,
        of interpretation,
      either as to meaning or intent.

My servants who seek know that of which I speak,
    know the methods of delivery,
    know the speed of information,
    know the pipeline to the stars,
    know the pipeline to the heavens,
    know the pipeline of confirmation which carries to and fro."

Eze 15:2 "Son of man, how is the wood of the vine *better* than any other wood, the vine branch which is among the trees of the forest?
Divine Commentary—

"My servants are not sought as slaves to instruction,
    as slaves of imprisonment,
    as slaves of compulsion,
    as slaves lacking comprehension,
    as slaves with ears that do not hear,
    as slaves with eyes which do not see,
    as slaves with a minimal relationship to the master who they
        seek to serve.

My servants are rewarded for their efforts,
    are rewarded for their lives of devotion,
    are rewarded as carriers of the truth,
    are rewarded for sharing access to the water of life,
    are rewarded for their Faith,
    are rewarded as their treasure stores beyond the grave."

Eze 15:3 "Is wood taken from it to make any object? Or can *men* make a peg from it to hang any vessel on?
Divine Commentary—

"My servants are invitees into a partnership with God,
    are adoptees into The Family of God,

are instated into the household of God.

My servants serve within their own freewill.
My servants attend at their own freewill.
My servants pray within their own freewill.
My servants seek within their own freewill.
My servants worship within their own freewill.

The slave of God does not know freewill,
        does not dwell upon The Earth,
        does not dwell within the heavens.

The slave of God is close-quartered,
        is enslaved by his soul,
        is there because of choice.

The slave of Satan has surrendered his freewill for what he has perceived as
        the bargain of the day,
        the bargain of the night,
        the bargain for his soul.

The slave of Satan has a future open to prediction."

Eze 15:4 "Instead, it is thrown into the fire for fuel; the fire devours both ends of it, and its middle is burned. Is it useful for *any* work?
Divine Commentary—

"My servants are supposed to open doors,
        to usher their companions through into a new beginning,
        to uphold and to teach The Edifice of God.

My servants are expected to expound all they have been taught of God,
        all they have acquired in truth,
        all which comprises a testimony of new life.

My servants are encouraged,
My servants are enlivened,
My servants are assisted by the availability of the tools of My Spirit,
        the gifts of My Spirit,
        the signs of My Spirit,
        the presence of My Spirit."

Eze 15:5 "Indeed, when it was whole, no object could be made from it. How much less will it be useful for *any* work when the fire has devoured it, and it is burned?
Divine Commentary—

"My servants change as they assimilate,
        change as they practise,
        change as they witness the works of God wherein they are placed.

My servants change in stature within their calling,
> change as evil is encountered,
> change as demons are seen to flee.

My servants change in confidence,
> change in appreciation,
> change in ability to lead:
>> as each grows a circle of experience around his soul and spirit.

My servants then seek the difficult,
> the advanced,
> the tasks that carry challenge,
> the environments with rulers enthroned on the high places.

My servants of supremacy know the power of prayer,
> know the marshalling of forces,
> know the storming of the citadels of darkness,
> know how to liberate a landscape from those who hold
>> the captives."

Eze 15:6 "Therefore thus says the Lord GOD: 'Like the wood of the vine among the trees of the forest, which I have given to the fire for fuel, so I will give up the inhabitants of Jerusalem;

Divine Commentary—

"My servants of supremacy do not venture anywhere without their armour,
> do not venture forth without their mantle,
> do not venture into territories anew without the approval of
>> their God.

My servants of supremacy can activate echelons of angels,
> can marshal the hosts of Heaven,
> can structure a battle so victory is assured,
> can call on the storms of My Spirit to fill the eyes of man,
> can call on the artillery of My Spirit to clear the battlefield of
>> Satanic forces.

My servants have at their disposal the might,
> the power,
> the authority,
>> to bind on Earth,
>> to loose on Earth,
> all which they choose to establish in The Name above all names.

My servants are encouraged to so unleash the power of God,
>> such that Satan vacates his throne,
>> in the areas so despoiled by centuries of neglect:
>> through the ignorance of the day."

Divine Intent— Ezekiel Ch 16

Scribal Note: *There are no specific divine commentaries on the content verses within this chapter.*

Upon enquiry of The Spirit as to the absence of such commentaries on Ezekiel Ch 16, The Lord shares His divine intent on this chapter:

"So Ezekiel is here given knowledge of the birthing,
of the development,
of the growth of Jerusalem:
of the apple of the eye of The Lord;
of the apple with a rotten core;
of the fruit of the tree of grandeur;
of the city with eternity in its grasp.

For in these days has My covenant been re-established,
is My atonement on the record,
is Grace within the footfalls of My city."

My Content Study Aid

Divine Intent— Ezekiel Ch 17

Scribal Note: *There are no specific divine commentaries on the content verses within this chapter.*

Upon enquiry of The Spirit as to the absence of such commentaries on Ezekiel Ch 17, The Lord shares His divine intent on this chapter:

"I speak to My Prophet Ezekiel with a message still to be learnt by My land of Israel,
>now restored before the nations of The Earth.

Behold!
Beware!
Stand Fast!

The King with his princes in Jerusalem still would strike hands with those which are oily,
>with those with
>>a slippery grip,
>with those equipped to lie
>>to all outside their Faith.

Stand Fast!

The King with his princes in Jerusalem would negate the wars upon My land,
>would negate the blood shed upon My land,
>would negate the victories with ink upon a pen."

My Content Study Aid

_____
_____
_____
_____
_____
_____
_____
_____
_____
_____
_____
_____
_____
_____

Divine Intent— Ezekiel Ch 18

Scribal Note*: There are no specific divine commentaries on the content verses within this chapter.*

Upon enquiry of The Spirit as to the absence of such commentaries on Ezekiel Ch 18, The Lord shares His divine intent on this chapter:

"As Ezekiel,
   My prophet,
   received My word,
   so the souls which sin shall die—
               both when within the law encased in their wicked ways,
               both when without the covering of Grace readily available—
                   without repentance from a blood-bathed heart.

For the transgressions of Israel still bring destruction on their heads for the sins they carry:
          as they continue waiting for The Saviour,
              The Messiah,
              The I AM,
                 long since come and gone.

For they still continue shouting for 'Barabbas' in their hearts as the message lies upon the dust,
          unaccepted by the sinful souls who wail.

For they still continue in their choice of remaining under law and with the chasing of good works.

For they still have their backs turned on the benevolence of Grace."

My Content Study Aid

_____
_____
_____
_____
_____
_____
_____
_____

Divine Commentary— Ezekiel Ch 19

Eze 19:1 "Moreover take up a lamentation for the princes of Israel,
Divine Commentary—

"My servants rarely know the end from the beginning,
      rarely can foresee the ramifications of their effort,
      rarely can attend a dedication arising from their vision.

My servants are not forgotten in the context within which they have served,
      are not forgotten where it matters,
      are not forgotten for the days of labour.

My servants do not have their rewards usurped by another,
      do not have their rewards overwritten by those who follow,
      do not have their rewards fail to make it to their store of treasure,
      do not have their rewards lose their sparkle or their pleasure,
      do not feel disappointment at a deferment of reward."

Eze 19:2 "and say: 'What *is* your mother? A lioness: She lay down among the lions;
Among the young lions she nourished her cubs.
Divine Commentary—

"My servants vacate,
My servants release,
My servants farewell as My Spirit counsels,
      as My Spirit completes,
      as My Spirit closes the reason for the presence of My servants.

My servants are not agents of deception,
      do not abuse the trust implicit in The Cross,
      do not carry items they would hide from The Light of day.

My servants value their integrity—
      of body,
      soul and spirit.

My servants do not despoil the status of their calling,
      the honour of their task,
      the beauty of their body.

My servants are careful in promoting,
      are watchful in their actions,
      are wise in their opinions.

My servants are careful in associating,
      are cautious in partnering,
      are trusting as verified.

My servants avoid the stigma of disgrace,
        avoid contamination by their peers,
        avoid the rumour and the lie.

My servants walk with precision in the narrow ways of God,
        shy from the crowded jostling on the runways of temptation."

Eze 19:3 She brought up one of her cubs, And he became a young lion; He learned to catch prey, And he devoured men.
Divine Commentary—
"My servants take their tools into the marketplace of man.
My servants support themselves within the marketplace of man.
My servants spread their abilities within the marketplace of man.

My servants seek equilibrium attuned to the marketplace of man.
My servants seek recompense from the marketplace of man.
My servants seek My provisioning only when failed by the marketplace of man.

My servants seeking their needs from within the marketplace of man do not feed from the
        table of The Lord.

For as My servants sow in disbelief so shall they reap in disbelief,
        so shall they become the beggars of The Lord,
        so shall they become beggared by the marketplace
        of man."

Eze 19:4 The nations also heard of him; He was trapped in their pit, And they brought him with chains to the land of Egypt.
Divine Commentary—
"My servants should not preach in hypocrisy,
        should not teach in hypocrisy,
        should not live in hypocrisy.

My servants should not be servants of hypocrisy with
        a sponge to placate the spirit and the soul,
        a sponge to mop the stains upon the heart,
        a sponge to blur the black spots into grey,
        a sponge called to mute the witness of a lie
        said to be the white of purity.

My servants should beware of a lie of any colour.

My servants should know the origin of a lie,
        the destiny of a liar,
        the lie made palatable by addition of an adjective which does
        not bear the truth."

Eze 19:5 'When she saw that she waited, *that* her hope was lost, She took another of her

cubs *and* made him a young lion.
Divine Commentary—

"My servants have their trinkets,
My servants have their addictions,
My servants have their idols:
    all hidden under names affording comfort in denial of reality."

Eze 19:6 He roved among the lions, And became a young lion; He learned to catch prey; He devoured men.
Divine Commentary—

"My servants hide behind a veneer as a mask upon a face,
    as a veil draped from a headdress:
    as righteousness is qualified,
        is partitioned,
        is divided,
        is torn into segments of convenience.

So too does righteousness have white co-mingled with the black,
    have a standard of greyness against which to match a life,
    have a standard which precludes inclusion with The Bride:
        when the drafting gate is used,
        when the mercy seat is covered,
        when Grace has been foregone."

Eze 19:7 He knew their desolate places, And laid waste their cities; The land with its fullness was desolated By the noise of his roaring.
Divine Commentary—

"My servants think their hearts are hidden,
    think the behaviour they deem private stays within a closet,
    think the shame is well and truly hidden,
    think the consequences will not be seen as relevant,
    think the sin is not—
        when called another name.

My servants err in thinking with,
    err in applying,
        the mindset of man:
        would put a cloak upon activities which are withheld from man.

My servants err in thinking such is also true with God,
        as when before His servants with knowledge to the fore,
        as when stood before An Altar of Holiness to The Lord,
        as when before selection for His Bride."

Eze 19:8 Then the nations set against him from the provinces on every side, And spread their net over him; He was trapped in their pit.
Divine Commentary—

"My servants have no escape when repentance is foregone,
> when there is unwillingness to change,
> when addiction wins the day,
> when Satan adds to his tally a soul yet in disguise.

Foolish are My servants to ignore that which they do not wish to hear,
> that which causes My Spirit to convict,
> > that which adulterates the morality of what was once a
> > > new born sheep.

My servants,
> more than most,
> > know the penalty for sin in all its variations.

My servants,
> more than most,
> > know to repent while it still is today."

Eze 19:9 They put him in a cage with chains, And brought him to the king of Babylon; They brought him in nets, That his voice should no longer be heard on the mountains of Israel.

Divine Commentary—

"My servants can be removed by man,
> can be removed by God,
> > can be removed for the benefit of My servants,
> > > for the benefit of My people,
> > > for the benefit of My place and time.

My servants can be silenced by man,
> can be silenced by God,
> can be silenced by themselves.

My servants who are silent may find it difficult to serve,
> may find it a new experience,
> may find it welcome as a habit.

My servants who are sated may find new fare difficult to stomach,
> may find new fare flaring on the tongue,
> may find new fare requiring a lot of grinding by the teeth
> > prior to understanding.

My servants who are hungry attend to new fare with enthusiasm,
> approach new fare willingly with acceptance,
> note the tingle of new fare upon the lips,
> adjust the taste of recognition as new fare rests upon the tongue,
> swallow new fare with ease when My Spirit does approve,
> receive new fare willingly which feeds their spirit and their soul."

Eze 19:10 'Your mother *was* like a vine in your bloodline, Planted by the waters,

Fruitful and full of branches Because of many waters.
Divine Commentary—

"My servants have a birthplace of remembrance,
      have a family with a story,
            a birth line of completion without a missing member.

My servants are each of their mother of the year,
            the descent line of establishment,
            the interwoven line of the birthing of new life,
                  of the maturing of that life,
                        of a new covenant with the Loving God who
                              walked with the forbears of the lines.

My servants are not isolated,
      are not encapsulated,
      are not oppressed,
            by time.

My servants know time as a period of Grace:
            a springboard to the heavens,
            a springboard to reunions,
            a springboard to the activities of the ages,
            a springboard to the wonders yet to be displayed before
                                  their eyes,
            a springboard to understanding of the origin of the life forces
                              inherent in the mortality of man,
            a springboard which uncoils the springtime of man's youth in
                              the presence of His God."

Eze 19:11 She had strong branches for sceptres of rulers. She towered in stature above the thick branches, And was seen in her height amid the dense foliage.
Divine Commentary—

"My servants know the heads of families,
      acknowledge the heads of families,
      care for the heads of families,
      support the heads of families.

My servants uphold the mantle borne by the heads of families,
                by a King-in-waiting,
                by a prince of the realm of Heaven,
                by a child of God adopted into the Household
                                  of Faith.

My servants do not vie for position,
      do not make order of importance,
      do not seek pre-eminence of standing.

My servants are destined as the eminences of eternity.

My servants are the glow plugs of ignition,
> the motors of the movement,
> the drivers of success,
> the harvesters with knowledge of the season."

Eze 19:12 But she was plucked up in fury, She was cast down to the ground, And the east wind dried her fruit. Her strong branches were broken and withered; The fire consumed them.
Divine Commentary—

"My servants know the songs of My Spirit,
> the languages of Heaven,
> encounter the discourses of man.

My servants know the futility of man when reliant on his own resources,
> know the thirst of man when he discovers a new resource,
> know the greed of man who does not want to share,
> know the fire of God which lingers on the horizon of man."

Eze 19:13 And now she *is* planted in the wilderness, In a dry and thirsty land.
Divine Commentary—

"My servants know the aching for lost souls,
> where the water does not long quench the thirst,
> where the dust of The Earth swirls within the habitations of man,
> where the whirlpools of the demons are at home with man,
> where the demons of the night greet the demons of the day,
> where the demons of the devil laugh and jeer at man.

My servants are charged to change the environment of man to be in favour with The God they choose to serve."

My Content Study Aid

Divine Commentary— Ezekiel Ch 20

Eze 20:1 It came to pass in the seventh year, in the fifth *month,* on the tenth *day* of the month, *that* certain of the elders of Israel came to inquire of the LORD, and sat before me.
Divine Commentary—

"My servants are aware of a time of enquiry,
        of a time of selection,
              of a time of penitence before The Lord.

My servants are aware of a time of sin,
        of a time of salvation,
              of a time of reconciliation.

My servants are aware of a time of baptism,
        of a time of Faith,
              of a time of covenant."

Eze 20:2 Then the word of the LORD came to me, saying,
Divine Commentary—

"My servants are aware of a time of loneliness,
        of a time of companionship,
              of a time of discipleship.

My servants are aware of a time of stunting,
        of a time of growth,
              of a time of fellowship.

My servants are aware of a time of entry,
        of a time of learning,
              of a time of departure."

Eze 20:3 "Son of man, speak to the elders of Israel, and say to them, 'Thus says the Lord GOD: "Have you come to inquire of Me? *As* I live," says the Lord GOD, "I will not be inquired of by you." '
Divine Commentary—

"My servants are aware of a time of a beginning,
        of a time of Grace,
              of an eternal time of projection.

My servants are aware of a time of a decision,
        of a time of judgment,
              of an eternal time of Hell.

My servants are aware of a time of offering,
        of a time of dedication,

of a time of confirmation.

My servants are aware of the set times of God."

Eze 20:12 "Moreover I also gave them My Sabbaths, to be a sign between them and Me, that they might know that I *am* the LORD who sanctifies them.
As in My book—
"As it is written so it is sustained.
   Every seventh day is still reserved as Holy unto The Lord,
      and this sign shall be upheld in honour by My servants,
                    My labourers—
                        all those professing,
                            with The Spirit on their lips,
                            and,
                            with their tongues,
                            declaring that Jesus is LORD."

Divine Commentary—

"My servants come before,
        attend to,
        worship at,
                The Altar of The Lord,
                The Altar of The Lamb,
                The Altar of The Son."

Eze 20:13 "Yet the house of Israel rebelled against Me in the wilderness; they did not walk in My statutes; they despised My judgments, 'which, *if* a man does, he shall live by them'; and they greatly defiled My Sabbaths. Then I said I would pour out My fury on them in the wilderness, to consume them.
Divine Commentary—

"My servants no longer suffer the rigidity of the law of sacrifice.

My servants now know the reconciliation born of Grace.

My servants now live under The Cross of sacrifice.

My servants now are bestowed the gifts of My Spirit.

My servants now dwell in a time of preparation."

Eze 20:14 "But I acted for My name's sake, that it should not be profaned before the Gentiles, in whose sight I had brought them out.
Divine Commentary—

"My servants do not see Me profane My Name,
        do not see My wrath as an embarrassment to My word,
        do not see their God acting within the demands of the day.

My servants do not see their God assessing right and wrong within the worldliness
                                                      of man."

Eze 20:43 "And there you shall remember your ways and all your doings with which you were defiled; and you shall loathe yourselves in your own sight because of all the evils that you have committed.
Divine Commentary—

"My servants when they sin should be familiar with My words to the Elders.

My servants when they sin dwell with their life in peril,
> dwell with their destiny at risk,
>> dwell at risk of suspension of their calling of My Spirit and
>>> their tasking of The Lord.

My servants in their sin are in urgent need of confession,
> are in urgent need of reconciliation,
> are in urgent need to forswear the devil's work."

Eze 20:44 "Then you shall know that I *am* the LORD, when I have dealt with you for My name's sake, not according to your wicked ways nor according to your corrupt doings, O house of Israel," says the Lord GOD.' "
Divine Commentary—

"My servants are not sacrificed from a high tower in an arid place,
> are not left as a huddled heap of failure in the dust,
> are not regarded as of little hope with their lifelines cut.

My servants learn from their experience,
> forsake the cause of injury,
> forsake the beam implanted in the eye,
> forsake the blockage embedded in the ear.

My servants are carried until they choose to stand again,
> until their limbs are straightened,
> until their spirits rise in conquest,
> until their souls rejoice before The Coming King.

My servants are redeemed by the utterance of their lips as driven by their tongue.
My servants are redeemed by the covenant written on their hearts.
My servants are redeemed by The Grace of God."

Eze 20:45 Furthermore the word of the LORD came to me, saying,
Divine Commentary—

"My servants are redeemed by The Grace of The Father,
> by the love of The Lord,
> by the testimony of My Spirit of their aching hearts."

Eze 20:46 "Son of man, set your face toward the south; preach against the south and prophesy against the forest land, the South,
Divine Commentary—

"My servants in the gathering of The Saints prophesy within the word of God,

> by the word of God,
> through the word of God.

My servants lead,
> direct and preach as instructed By My Spirit;
> lead,
> direct and preach as their words flow from My Spirit;
> lead,
> direct and preach:
>> in order the signs of The Kingdom are evident within the assemblies
>> of The Saints of The Living God.

My servants are not easily dismissed,
> are appointed with wisdom,
> are sustained by fellowship with God,
> are graduated with honour from the tenure of their tasking."

My Content Study Aid

_____
_____
_____
_____
_____
_____
_____
_____
_____
_____
_____
_____
_____
_____
_____
_____
_____
_____
_____
_____

Divine Commentary— Ezekiel Ch 21

Eze 21:1 And the word of the LORD came to me, saying,
Divine Commentary—

"My servants who are in a relationship of sincerity will know the pipeline of sincerity,
        will know the pipeline of conversation,
        will know the pipeline of query and response,
        will know the pipeline of gratitude and confirmation,
        will know the pipeline as a conduit of The Will of God,
                of the tasking of The Lord,
                of the counsel of The Spirit:
            as the transmission line of The Loving God set up as a
                linkage to the components of the mind of man."

Eze 21:2 "Son of man, set your face toward Jerusalem, preach against the holy places, and prophesy against the land of Israel;
Divine Commentary—

"My servant who serves with wisdom and understanding serves the perfect will of God:
        as he looks continuously for the leading of My Spirit,
                the confirmation of My Spirit,
                the counsel of My Spirit."

Eze 21:3 "and say to the land of Israel, 'Thus says the LORD: "Behold, I *am* against you, and I will draw My sword out of its sheath and cut off both righteous and wicked from you.
Divine Commentary—

"My servant knows when to stand within his covering,
    knows when to advance to overcome,
    knows when the captive is set free.

My servant knows the power and the authority within which he is designated to move,
            within which he is designated to administer,
            within which he is designated to
                acknowledge with thankfulness for
                the outpouring of the works of God."

Eze 21:4 "Because I will cut off both righteous and wicked from you, therefore My sword shall go out of its sheath against all flesh from south *to* north,
Divine Commentary—

"My servant who does not know his calling,
    who does not recall the vision,
    who does not know the limits of his jurisdiction:
        is as a snowflake in a tempest carried it knows not where,
            dropped upon an unprepared landscape,

> subjected to a random walk within an
> avalanche of turmoil.

My servant is then at risk in all he does,
> in all he sees,
> in all his relationships within a quest for success.

My servant is then at the mercy of the onset of frustration,
> of the onset of disappointment,
> at the onset of embitterment for his failure on the field of battle.

My servant may then fall as a casualty of a conflict which he never understood:
> from which he may be wounded with a fiery dart,
> from which he may not return with honour,
> from which he never was assigned by his loving God."

Eze 21:5 "that all flesh may know that I, the LORD, have drawn My sword out of its sheath; it shall not return anymore." '
Divine Commentary—

"My servants know how to hack and harry,
> know how to chip and shatter,
> know how to bind and loose.

My servants know their weapons of dissolution,
> know their weapons of dissipation:
> know their weapons of the tongue.

My servants know the boldness of My Spirit,
> The Faith which destroys a fortress,
> My word which brings an empire to its knees."

Eze 21:6 "Sigh therefore, son of man, with a breaking heart, and sigh with bitterness before their eyes.
Divine Commentary—

"My servant goes with a loving heart,
> does all he does in love,
> knows the compassion of his soul.

My servant sees the pall of bitterness,
> the approaching gloom,
> the outline of a death.

My servant also blinks at a tear which surfaces,
> at a tear founded on a memory,
> at a tear unbidden—
> > to fall as a teardrop from an eye which weeps.

My servant knows compassion within the circumstance of man.

My servant knows to offer solace to the soul,
>> comfort to the spirit.

My servant knows of the need for fellowship in a time of trial."

Eze 21:7 "And it shall be when they say to you, 'Why are you sighing?' that you shall answer, 'Because of the news; when it comes, every heart will melt, all hands will be feeble, every spirit will faint, and all knees will be weak *as* water. Behold, it is coming and shall be brought to pass,' says the Lord GOD."
Divine Commentary—

"My servants know the sound of trumpets,
>> know the music of the dirge.

My servants hear the good news of salvation,
>> hear the distraught news arising from a prophecy.

My servants use the time of warning to protect from the time of desperation."

Eze 21:8 Again the word of the LORD came to me, saying,
Divine Commentary—

"My servants seek answers to problems of the moment,
>> seek solutions to difficulties of the hour,
>> seek counsel as to how to overcome the contents of a day.

Those who seek their God of Love are never turned away with nothing on their tongue."

Eze 21:9 "Son of man, prophesy and say, 'Thus says the LORD!' Say: 'A sword, a sword is sharpened And also polished!
Divine Commentary—

"My servants meld My word,
>> recompose My word,
>> select My word:
>>> as a tribute to comprehension,
>>> as a tribute to the market place,
>>> as a tribute to the search by man,
>>> as a tribute to the bending of the truth,
>>> as a tribute of interpretation to soften the ears of man,
>>> as a tribute to the waywardness of man.

My servants know these aspects of My word too well,
>> practise these aspects of My word too well,
>> produce to a schedule these aspects of My word:
>>> these,
>>>> the epitaphs of their ministries,
>>>>> of their tasking,
>>>>> of the validity of a vision,
>>>>> of a calling from The Lord.

My servants too well-know of books of income designed to tickle ears;
>are as wafers with no filling,
>>with no fresh content worth perusal,
>>with no substance worth the price.

For as the content of a waffle scarcely impacts on the feeding of a life,
>so the waffle which surrounds My word neither feeds the spirit nor the soul.

My servants would show wisdom to revisit that of which they do without referral
>for approval."

Eze 21:10 Sharpened to make a dreadful slaughter, Polished to flash like lightning! Should we then make mirth? It despises the sceptre of My son, *As it does* all wood. Divine Commentary—

"My servants sharpen their abilities,
>polish their memory of recall,
>establish their resources to the fore.

My servants should know the season in which they mature,
>the season of their labour,
>the season of their rest.

My servants should not imperil the basis of their health.

My servants should not procure the gimmicks of the market place,
>the items produced for the gullible,
>the discoveries with claims which have no standing with respect,
>the pitfalls of a pseudo-science which medicates the body without
>>oversight or recourse.

My servants should beware of the knaves which are at home within the market place
>of man."

My Content Study Aid

_____
_____
_____
_____
_____
_____
_____
_____

Divine Commentary— Ezekiel Ch 22

Eze 22:1 Moreover the word of the LORD came to me, saying,
Divine Commentary—

"My servants are diligent in application,
> are diligent in their seeking,
> are diligent in bearing,
>> for repair,
>>> the body of man before the throne of God.

My servants seek perfection prematurely in an imperfect world.

My servants seek completion of all they ask and do.

My servants seek the knowledge which guarantees success.

My servants sometimes seek to usurp the freewill of God,
> to deny God His freewill in favour of a request,
> to impose constraints which will ensure the outcome
>> they desire."

Eze 22:2 "Now, son of man, will you judge, will you judge the bloody city? Yes, show her all her abominations!
Divine Commentary—

"My servants validate their efforts by their measure of success.

My servants succumb to error in measuring the flesh.

My servants show wisdom when they validate the spirit and the soul,
> when they validate the presence of My Spirit in a life,
> when they validate the confession of the supremacy of
>> The God of Love in body,
>>> soul and spirit.

My servants do the greater good in attending to the welfare of a spirit and a soul,
> of praying for unison between the spirit and the soul,
> of checking on the health signs of the spirit,
>> on the sin signs of the soul,
> of how the body is reacting to an environment in
>> which it is forced to dwell."

Eze 22:3 "Then say, 'Thus says the Lord GOD: "The city sheds blood in her own midst, that her time may come; and she makes idols within herself to defile herself.
Divine Commentary—

"My servants encounter the curdling signage of the conurbations,
> encounter the erection of the idols,
> encounter the offerings as tendered to the resin and the stone.

My servants pause in the presence of each encounter—
> to throw the pillars down,
> to dismiss the effigies of idolatry,
> to address the demonic powers so boldly on display:
>> that they may not stand with immunity as an image of satanic force,
>>> of satanic influence,
>>> of satanic capture,
>>> of satanic thrones which lie in wait,
>>> of satanic nightmares of corruption,
>>> of satanic structures blending
>>>> animals with man.

My servants are to confront the demonic with My Spirit,
> to confront the profane with the sacred,
> to confront the effigies with the truth:
>> in a prayer of desolation which binds,
>>> pulls down,
>>> lays waste the influence,
>>>> the positioning,
>>>> the status acknowledged by man:
>>>>> to the presented works of Satan."

Eze 22:4 "You have become guilty by the blood which you have shed, and have defiled yourself with the idols which you have made. You have caused your days to draw near, and have come to *the end of* your years; therefore I have made you a reproach to the nations, and a mockery to all countries.

Divine Commentary—

"My servants walk among the idols of the nations with tongues which do not speak,
> with tongues uncommitted to the
>> power of declaration,
> with tongues not conversant with
>> My Spirit.

My servants fail in their professed belief,
> fail in their integrity of performance,
> fail in their de facto acceptance of the status quo.

My servants walk a walk where idols are treated as sacrosanct,
> where idols are bypassed without a second glance,
> where idols dot the landscapes of the devil.

My servants are unaware of when they are walking in a battlefield,
> do not recognise the enemy when encountered,
> would rather continue on their way with their souls untroubled.

My servants are accountable for idols they see yet do not engage,
> idols they visit yet ignore,

idols they meet yet do not confront,
idols active in the night yet over such they do not shed
The Light,
idols of confrontation yet from such they choose to
shy away,
idols active in the national cultures yet they accept such
without a murmur of dissent."

Eze 22:5 "*Those* near and *those* far from you will mock you as infamous *and* full of tumult.
Divine Commentary—

"My servants have the knowledge to free captives from the imposition stemming from
the gaol of history,
from the history of ignorance which
still pervades the present,
from the culture developed upon gods
of no impact on the reality of life.

My servants come to speak of The God which is not surrendered to participate in a lie,
of The God which is active in their lives,
of The God of Truth,
of Love,
of Healing,
of Discipleship with honour,
of eternal life with understanding.

My servants know The God throughout the ages,
The God of prophecy,
The God of commitment to His creation,
The God of sacrifice for the benefit of His peoples,
The God with a covenant with man which is upheld before all the
peoples of The Earth,
The God who offers Grace for the salvation of man,
The God who died as a sacrifice for man.

My servants welcome The Multitudes into the presence of the unique and loving God
who practises forgiveness in desiring a relationship with man,
the unique and truthful God who claims to be the only way for man
to enter into His Presence with eternal life,
the unique and all powerful God who is the creator of the universe,
the namer of the stars,
the commissioner of
His Holy Spirit:
to dwell within His saints as their counsellor,
as the guide established to lead His people home."

Eze 22:6 "Look, the princes of Israel: each one has used his power to shed blood in you.

Divine Commentary—

"My servants do not shed the blood of the living,
    do not shed the blood of the dying,
    neither gather nor spill the blood of the dead.

My servants know the blood of man is sacred unto life,
    is now in no need of further sacrifice,
    is not to be laid upon an altar,
    was once and for all spilt upon a cross.

My servants know of the recompense for sin,
    of the price already paid,
    of adoption into The Family of God.

My servants praise and worship The Living God—
    The Loving God who honours life,
    The Loving God who honours women,
    The Loving God who honours the marriage bed of man."

Eze 22:7 "In you they have made light of father and mother; in your midst they have oppressed the stranger; in you they have mistreated the fatherless and the widow.
Divine Commentary—

"My servants experience the uniqueness of Jesus The Christ,
    the uniqueness of His teachings,
    the uniqueness of His life,
    the uniqueness of His rising from the grave,
    the uniqueness of the testimonies,
    the uniqueness of the witnesses down through the ages—
    who did not forsake their testimonies even unto tortured deaths:
        the martyrs of The Cross."

My Content Study Aid

Divine Intent— Ezekiel Ch 23

Scribal Note*: There are no specific divine commentaries on the content verses within this chapter.*

Upon enquiry of The Spirit as to the absence of such commentaries on Ezekiel Ch 23, The Lord shares His divine intent on this chapter:

"Ezekiel,
   My prophet,
      records My word to him concerning the cities of Samaria and of Jerusalem
         with their growth from their youth unto maturity,
         their growth in harlotry,
          in adultery,
           in lewdness:
  as I,
    The Lord,
      alienated Myself from the presence of their sins until
             righteousness prevails.

So this has relevance,
   even so as Ezekiel declared,
   to the end-times of this age of Grace:
        as Jerusalem takes vengeance unto herself on Palestine;
        as forgiveness is a stranger to her heart;
        as she knows not the God of Grace;
           so she shall know that I am The Lord GOD."

My Content Study Aid

_____
_____
_____
_____
_____
_____
_____
_____
_____
_____

Divine Commentary— Ezekiel Ch 24

Eze 24:1 Again, in the ninth year, in the tenth month, on the tenth *day* of the month, the word of the LORD came to me, saying,
Divine Commentary—

"My servants celebrate the word of God,
        celebrate the new day,
        celebrate the coming into life,
        celebrate the ministry of God,
        celebrate the promises of God,
        celebrate the new covenant in force.

My servants celebrate in service to their God.

My servants celebrate in words of acclamation,
        in words of testimony,
            in words poorly describing their witnessing of miracles.

My servants celebrate the rescues,
        celebrate in gratitude,
        celebrate renewals,
        celebrate the impact of The Cross,
        celebrate the compassion for a child.

My servants celebrate the changing of a life,
        celebrate the removal of a burden,
        celebrate the freedom from a fear,
        celebrate a new beginning,
        celebrate the peace of God.

My servants celebrate in The Grace of God,
        in the healing power of God,
        in the relationship with God.

My servants celebrate the joy within discovery of all their God does do."

Eze 24:2 "Son of man, write down the name of the day, this very day—the king of Babylon started his siege against Jerusalem this very day.
Divine Commentary—

"My servants tread the stairway to success,
        the stairway to companionship,
        the stairway to a faithful destiny.

My servants tread in footsteps of certain placement,
        in footsteps without an echo,
        in footsteps which encounter new levels:
            each with their vista of opportunity—

>   where the railings of the stairwell provide support of access to
>   the vista which deserves more than a hurried glance.

My servants know the stairway to the heavens is extremely well lit,
> with the treads securely fixed,
> with branching stairs fully signed as to the means of access,
>> as to the purpose of the prayer,
>> as to the function of the stairs,
>> as to the destination disclosed.

My servants are in wonder at the staircase to the heavens,
> at the complexity of options which open before the eyes,
> at the rewards of service as height improves the view,
> at the input of wisdom for the feeding of the spirit and
>> the soul,
> at the traffic on the staircase which treads the steps with joy."

Eze 24:3 "And utter a parable to the rebellious house, and say to them, 'Thus says the Lord GOD: "Put on a pot, set *it* on, And also pour water into it.
Divine Commentary—

"My servants serve the search of victory to the seekers of a purpose,
> serve the search of victory to those imprisoned by their fears,
> serve the search of victory to the down-trodden,
>> to the pain-bearers,
>> to the downcast souls.

My servants serve the search of victory to the lost within the maze of life,
> to the fearful within the jungles of despair,
> to the wistful who dream of a better way,
> to the hurried and the harried who long for a
>> peaceful rest,
> to the busy and the bashful unable to give voice
>> to their desires.

My servants serve the search of victory already mixed with the recipe for success,
> already stirred and shaken to sate the palate of
>> the tongue,
> already screened in fulness of the truth to satisfy
>> the knowing and the wise,
> already prepared to bring a message to the weak
>> and the ill-informed."

Eze 24:4 Gather pieces *of meat* in it, Every good piece, The thigh and the shoulder. Fill *it* with choice cuts;
Divine Commentary—

"My servants gather the shards of broken pots to see the search of victory repair the
> broken and the shattered,

> to see the beauty of what 'once was'
> > restored again to fulness of
> > > the finished form,
> > to see history as it became change to
> > > become the future as
> > > > it is discerned.

> My servants know the shards of broken pots originating from the hands of man are as the
> > segments of a temple now resulting from the handiwork of God.

> For as the hands of man once held the perfection of his pot,
> > so The God of Heaven deemed perfection into His creation
> > > for a garden—
> > the spirit and the soul of man complete within his Temple.

> So The Temple of man is re-instated on The Earth."

Eze 24:5 Take the choice of the flock. Also pile *fuel* bones under it, Make it boil well, And let the cuts simmer in it."
Divine Commentary—

> "My servants encourage the quest for knowledge,
> > encourage the wonder of restoration,
> > > encourage the achieving of an intended destiny.

> My servants love their fellow man.

> My servants love their God.

> My servants love their callings,
> > with such as they are tasked to do."

Eze 24:7 For her blood is in her midst; She set it on top of a rock; She did not pour it on the ground, To cover it with dust.
Divine Commentary—

> "My servants see the Master approaching,
> > see the Master carrying a lamb,
> > see the Master searching back and forth,
> > see the Master extracting a goat from among the thorns,
> > see the Master carrying the lamb and the kid.

> My servants see the Master putting down the lamb,
> > putting down the kid,
> > > as He walks away.

> My servants see both the lamb and the kid skip and dance,
> > as they closely follow in the footprints of the Master.

> My servants see the Master pause,
> > turn,
> > call;

        see each of the hopefuls dash into His waiting arms.

My servants now see the Master,
                still searching,
        as He carries two lambs within His care."

Eze 24:8 That it may raise up fury and take vengeance, I have set her blood on top of a rock, That it may not be covered."
Divine Commentary—

"My servants know the goats of man may become the sheep of God when their coverings are replaced."

Eze 24:9 'Therefore thus says the Lord GOD: "Woe to the bloody city! I too will make the pyre great.
Divine Commentary—

"My servants are discrete in all they hear and see,
        in all they witness with The Lord,
        in all they encounter before the demons.

My servants hold a sacred trust,
    hold a holy calling,
    hold in all due reverence their God of the abundant life.

My servants know no rancour,
    know no jealousy,
    know no selfishness,
    know no envy,
    know no convicting reason for a furrowed brow.

My servants move in My ministry within the blessings of My Spirit,
                within the conquest by their tongues,
                within the confession of their Faith,
                within the blood of The Lamb,
                within the power of their testimonies."

Eze 24:10 Heap on the wood, Kindle the fire; Cook the meat well, Mix in the spices, And let the cuts be burned up.
Divine Commentary—

"My servants know the fuel which feeds the fire,
    know the purpose of the fire,
    know when it scorches but does not burn,
    know when it refines in purity of purpose to remove the dross.

My servants know the fuel of sin which besets the flesh of man."

Eze 24:24 'Thus Ezekiel is a sign to you; according to all that he has done you shall do; and when this comes, you shall know that I *am* the Lord GOD.' "
As in My book—

'As it has been written now henceforth it comes,
> now to be fulfilled,
> > now to confirm the preparation of,
> > > the witness to,
> > > > The Lord.'

Eze 24:27 'On that day your mouth will be opened to him who has escaped; you shall speak and no longer be mute. Thus you will be a sign to them, and they shall know that I *am* the LORD.' "
As in My book—

'In that day it was written for a day such as this.

The Flame of Heaven will counsel those who labour in the vineyards,
> empowering with boldness those in the Kingdom of God:
> > that they may go forth declaring the Kingdom of God is nigh—
> > > and with power,
> > > and with authority,
> > > and with signs,
> > > and with wonders,
> > > and with miracles declaring the Word of The Lord,
> > > > with a certainty beyond their years,
> > > and with an impact beyond their present understanding.'

My Content Study Aid

_____
_____
_____
_____
_____
_____
_____
_____
_____
_____
_____
_____
_____
_____
_____
_____

Divine Commentary— Ezekiel Ch 25

Eze 25:1 The word of the LORD came to me, saying,
Divine Commentary—

"My servants trial and test in the attempts of man to discover The Will of God.

My servants sometimes act as if The Will of God is as an island in the sea
      awaiting discovery,
    is as an island with inviting shores,
    is as an island with unknown content in
      the hinterland,
    is as an island where water lies in
      waiting for a search of thirst,
    is as an island uninhabited by man,
    is as an island which is always difficult
      for man to find.

My servants often overlook,
    often forget to use,
    often forget to access,
    often forget to tender for confirmation,
      the wisdom inherent in the will of man being subject to The Will of God,
        being in companionship with My Spirit,
        being in a checkout which rings the
          register of God."

Eze 25:2 "Son of man, set your face against the Ammonites, and prophesy against them.
Divine Commentary—

"My servants often neither sift nor sieve all which forms the input to their lives,
    take in the spurious and the gloss placed for attraction,
    assimilate the rumour and the lie from a heap of discards,
    dress up the quest of vanity with words to disguise intent,
    preen and pout in mirrors which no longer reflect reality,
    scowl at and smudge the answers not met with satisfaction,
    linger at the lamp post awaiting change in where the shadows fall."

Eze 25:3 "Say to the Ammonites, 'Hear the word of the Lord GOD! Thus says the Lord GOD: "Because you said, 'Aha!' against My sanctuary when it was profaned, and against the land of Israel when it was desolate, and against the house of Judah when they went into captivity,
Divine Commentary—

"My servants do not scoff,
    are not sceptical of an uttered promise,
    should not desert their postings,

should not leave on an unbidden holiday at the expense of victory,
should not debate the inexact,
should not bring a tale of conflict into the house of God."

Eze 25:4 "indeed, therefore, I will deliver you as a possession to the men of the East, and they shall set their encampments among you and make their dwellings among you; they shall eat your fruit, and they shall drink your milk.
Divine Commentary—

"My servants are rewarded for all they say and do—
the rewards for being wise,
the rewards for being foolish.

My servants should not enact the invasion of insidiousness which brings false gods to
their shores,
false gods which are not sent fleeing home,
false gods which are comforted as a sign
of conciliation.

My servants tolerate Satan active on the battlefield,
do not anchor the efforts of their forbears,
do not realise how their Faith is watered down by impurities of installation,
of how a homeland is peppered with the seasoning from the
imports of the guests."

Eze 25:5 "And I will make Rabbah a stable for camels and Ammon a resting place for flocks. Then you shall know that I *am* the LORD."
Divine Commentary—

"My servants are called to stand before demonic activity,
before the idols of iniquity,
before the idolatry of man.

My servants are called to stand and to know the victory,
to stand and to advance against the foe,
to stand and to establish claim arising from a war."

Eze 25:6 'For thus says the Lord GOD: "Because you clapped *your* hands, stamped your feet, and rejoiced in heart with all your disdain for the land of Israel,
Divine Commentary—

"My servants shout for the rafters of support,
shout for the protection from the elements,
shout for the comfort of enclosure;
shout at the coming storm,
shout at the testing of the nations,
shout at the coming destruction buried within the climax.

My servants will hesitate and scurry,
will visit and depart,

        will stick and stay where they belong."

Eze 25:7 "indeed, therefore, I will stretch out My hand against you, and give you as plunder to the nations; I will cut you off from the peoples, and I will cause you to perish from the countries; I will destroy you, and you shall know that I *am* the LORD."
Divine Commentary—

"My servants neither void nor cancel their call to arms,
        neither hide nor hinder their force of arms,
        neither corrupt nor compromise the validity of their arms.

  For the arms of God are the repository for the arming of His servants.

  For as He sees His servants armed so will they charge in unison,
        so will the yelling of the word of God lay low the
                resolution of the enemy,
        so will the presence of My Banner deny the stand
                of demons,
        mark and endow with angels,
        proclaim and overcome in the
                presence of The Light.

My servants verify the vilifiers,
        despatch the despots of disdain,
        encircle the envelopers with the enlisted entities.

My servants know My sword of conquest,
        know My truth and light:
                those with their authority burnished by My blood once shed upon
                            The Earth.

My servants handle well their armour of the battle where the flesh is not at stake."

Eze 25:8 'Thus says the Lord GOD: "Because Moab and Seir say, 'Look! The house of Judah *is* like all the nations,'
Divine Commentary—

"My servants take and do not give,
        seize and do not yield,
        possess and do not retreat,
        gather and do not scatter:
                in the battle for the soul of man;
                in the battle for the spirit's life;
                in the battle where the powers of darkness are to be forced to flee.

My servants claim the spoils of war:
        the treasure chests of families complete and bearing fruit,
        the treasure chests of testimonies which can now be told and heard,
        the treasure chests of memories now fulfilled and can be shared,
        the treasure chests of souls now rescued and restored,

the treasure chests prevented from hurling from a cliff,
the treasure chests which were inundated by disease and destined for a pit,
the treasure chests now lifted up into a destiny of light."

Eze 25:9 "therefore, behold, I will clear the territory of Moab of cities, of the cities on its frontier, the glory of the country, Beth Jeshimoth, Baal Meon, and Kirjathaim.
Divine Commentary—

"My servants are on a journey filled with majesty,
are on a journey of very great significance,
are on a journey where The Kingdom of The Light clashes with
the embitterment of the ages:
the totality of evil—
for the eternal destiny of both the spirit and the soul of man."

Eze 25:10 "To the men of the East I will give it as a possession, together with the Ammonites, that the Ammonites may not be remembered among the nations.
Divine Commentary—

"My servants will witness the imprisonment of Satan,
the destruction of his jurisdiction,
the despatch of all who made him their figurehead of choice.

My servants witness the effects of his lies,
the effects of his plots of power,
the effects of his schemes of debt,
the effects of his oaths of blood,
the effects of his wars against the flesh of man,
the effects of his torturing of man,
the effects of his corrupting of man,
the effects of his depraving of man.

Satan with his cohorts will not yield in the presence with insecurity,
in the presence with embedded sin,
in the presence with a hook,
in the presence with no repentance."

Eze 25:11 "And I will execute judgments upon Moab, and they shall know that I *am* the LORD."
Divine Commentary—

"My servants are in the midst of the suffering of The Multitudes,
are in surroundings neither conducive to mercy nor forgiveness,
are in the localities of man where sin drags down the glory of man:
the freewill of man—
to be measured solely by his quest for survival.

My servants see the importance attached to man's instinct for survival,
attached to the life of man,
attached to his basic needs unfulfilled this day.

My servants see the breeding of the flies,
>> the rotting of the flesh;
>>> have their nostrils twitch at the stinking smell of death found in the heat
>>>> of day."

Eze 25:12 'Thus says the Lord GOD: "Because of what Edom did against the house of Judah by taking vengeance, and has greatly offended by avenging itself on them,"
Divine Commentary—

"My servants are aware of to whom the right to vengeance solely falls,
>> by whom vengeance should be wielded,
>>> for whom vengeance is the weapon of last resort after
>>>> warnings are ignored.

The day for the release of vengeance is reserved solely as the right,
>> as the property,
>>> as within the arsenal of God.

Foolish are they who appropriate the right to vengeance,
> who instigate the act of vengeance,
> who oversee,
> who lose control,
> who are unable to rescind,
>> the vengeance of the soul once unleashed by man."

Eze 25:13 'therefore thus says the Lord GOD: "I will also stretch out My hand against Edom, cut off man and beast from it, and make it desolate from Teman; Dedan shall fall by the sword.
Divine Commentary—

"My servants know the favour of The Lord,
> know the rebuke of The Lord.

My servants know The Fear of God as the governing directive in their lives,
>> as the governing attitude of approach,
>>> as the governing aspect of the character in submission
>>>> of assessment:
>>> the tribute offered as the base on which to build,
>>>> on which to enhance,
>>>>> a close relationship with God."

Eze 25:14 "I will lay My vengeance on Edom by the hand of My people Israel, that they may do in Edom according to My anger and according to My fury; and they shall know My vengeance," says the Lord GOD.
Divine Commentary—

"My servants neither desert nor flee The Will of God.

My servants offer hearts of rejoicing in the favour of The Lord.

My servants offer hearts of repentance at the rebuke of The Lord.

My servants do not sulk,
> are not surly,
>> at the directed word of God.

My servants give thanks in all things relating to their God of Love,
> to their God of Life,
> to their God which saves the penitent
>> from Hell,
>> from the claws of Satan,
>> from a destiny of eternal loss."

Eze 25:15 'Thus says the Lord GOD: "Because the Philistines dealt vengefully and took vengeance with a spiteful heart, to destroy because of the old hatred,"
Divine Commentary—

"My servants do not see their gowns of life within mortality.

My servants do not yet see their chests which store their treasures of redemption.

My servants do not yet know the magnificence of their treasure,
> the wonder of their treasure,
>> the measure of their treasure or of the opportunities which
>>> await beyond the grave of man.

My servants do not enquire into the mysteries of God.

My servants are content with that which God chooses to declare,
> chooses to make known,
> chooses to lay before the mind of man."

My Content Study Aid

Divine Intent— Ezekiel Ch 26

Scribal Note: *There are no specific divine commentaries on the content verses within this chapter.*

Upon enquiry of The Spirit as to the absence of such commentaries on Ezekiel Ch 26, The Lord shares His divine intent on this chapter:

"My word to Ezekiel still is bounded by application,
      still carries punishment for those sneering at Jerusalem,
      still will earn the lesson vested on Tyre.
  Beware,
    O Nations of The Earth—
      those who would sneer when Jerusalem suffers:
      those who would be wise beforehand to recall the fate of Tyre."

My Content Study Aid

Divine Commentary— Ezekiel Ch 27

Eze 27:1   The word of the LORD came again to me, saying,
Divine Commentary—

"My servants revisit episodes within their past:
        episodes of happiness,
        episodes of grief,
        episodes of honour,
        episodes of shame.

My servants revisit episodes of celebration,
        episodes of joy,
        episodes of amusement,
        episodes where work dominates a scene.

My servants revisit episodes where effort was rewarded,
        where effort was wasted as it fell upon a desert.

My servants recall their dramatic times with God which impact both the memory and
        the heart.

My servants recall the stories found within the harvest fields,
        the highlights in which Christ crossed their paths,
        the encounters with divine appointments where a soul was assisted
        into a new relationship."

Eze 27:2   "Now, son of man, take up a lamentation for Tyre,
Divine Commentary—

"My servants call out for the repetition of success,
        call out to see their God in action,
        call out for the freeing of the slave to poverty,
        call out for the opening of the door to freedom:
            the door of education,
            the door of enlightenment:
                which sets the world aflame with opportunity
                for the spirit and the soul of man."

Eze 27:3   "and say to Tyre, 'You who are situated at the entrance of the sea, merchant of the peoples on many coastlands, thus says the Lord GOD: "O Tyre, you have said, 'I *am* perfect in beauty.'
Divine Commentary—

"My servants give voice to their authority to command the downfall:
        of all who would bring the spirit of man unto oblivion,
        the soul of man unto imprisonment."

Eze 27:4   Your borders *are* in the midst of the seas. Your builders have perfected your beauty.

Divine Commentary—

"My servants give voice to Faith in action with the loosing of the oversight of God into a life.

My servants give voice to Faith in action with the binding of demonic activities within a life.

My servants give voice to Faith in action in service to The Living God."

Eze 27:5   They made all *your* planks of fir trees from Senir; They took a cedar from Lebanon to make you a mast.

Divine Commentary—

"My servants exhibit loyalty which underscores their freewill,
    exhibit knowledge which underscores their wisdom,
    exhibit perseverance which underscores their commitment.

My servants love and attend their God which underscores their relationship:
        their freshness of endeavour,
        their freshness of approach,
        their freshness of application.

My servants have bound the stakes of staleness,
    have bound the clothing of complacency,
    have bound the vine-wood of the forest.

My servants have thrown the stakes,
    the clothing,
    the vine-wood:
        onto the bonfire of My Spirit."

Eze 27:6   *Of* oaks from Bashan they made your oars; The company of Ashurites have inlaid your planks *With* ivory from the coasts of Cyprus

Divine Commentary—

"My servants count the cost prior to a commitment to proceed.

My servants know their liabilities,
    know the assets available for use.

My servants ensure My Spirit leads,
    My Spirit goes before,
    My Spirit carries the torch lit for the placing of the feet.

My servants enter through the opened doors,
    do not try the doors of closure."

Eze 27:7   Fine embroidered linen from Egypt was what you spread for your sail; Blue and purple from the coasts of Elishah was what covered you.

Divine Commentary—

"My servants contribute to the task in hand,
    contribute to the presentation,
    contribute with their testimonies,
    contribute to the truthfulness of the integrity of God.

My servants contribute as My Spirit confirms their actions of the day.

My servants contribute with their prayers which have the ear of God."

Eze 27:8 "Inhabitants of Sidon and Arvad were your oarsmen; Your wise men, O Tyre, were in you; They became your pilots.
Divine Commentary—

"My servants are aware of those who know the way in a distant land,
    of those who can lead and guide in the ways of man,
    of those who drive the camels of convenience across the
        landscape of the soul.

My servants are aware of those who know the tents of hospitality."

Eze 27:9 Elders of Gebal and its wise men Were in you to caulk your seams; All the ships of the sea And their oarsmen were in you To market your merchandise.
Divine Commentary—

"My servants offer but do not sell their wares,
    offer but do not sell their prayers,
    offer but do not sell the living water which brings new life to a
        thirsty soul."

Eze 27:10 "Those from Persia, Lydia, and Libya Were in your army as men of war; They hung shield and helmet in you; They gave splendour to you.
Divine Commentary—

"My servants draw the battle lines.

My servants dress in their armour.

My servants hold their weapons of My Spirit in readiness for use.

My servants dress My battlefield in the splendour of My Spirit."

Eze 27:11 Men of Arvad with your army *were* on your walls *all* around, And the men of Gammad were in your towers; They hung their shields on your walls *all* around; They made your beauty perfect.
Divine Commentary—

"My servants can visit in My Spirit,
    can visit in the reality of man:
        the battlefields of God.

The battlefields of God are wider,
    are more extensive,
        than the embattled defences of the devil with his
        demons in accord."

Eze 27:12 "Tarshish *was* your merchant because of your many luxury goods. They gave you silver, iron, tin, and lead for your goods.
Divine Commentary—

"My servants proclaim The Living God.

>I AM He who died The Son of Man and rose The Son of God.
>
>I AM He who died so man may live.
>
>I AM He who lives so man may inherit.
>
>I AM He who seeks the preparation of man.
>
>I AM He who welcomes man,
>>as committed to his journey,
>>>back home into My presence."

Eze 27:34 But you are broken by the seas in the depths of the waters; Your merchandise and the entire company will fall in your midst.
Divine Commentary—

"My servants witness the progressive fall of the foe of man,
>witness the progressive contraction of his areas of influence established
>>over centuries,
>
>witness the citadels of darkness wilt and melt before The Light,
>>before the word of God,
>>before My servants with their hosts,
>>before what their tongues proclaim,
>>before the collective prayers of
>>>My saints."

Eze 27:35 All the inhabitants of the isles will be astonished at you; Their kings will be greatly afraid, And *their* countenance will be troubled.
Divine Commentary—

"My servants surprise those with other gods,
>surprise those who know no gods,
>surprise those who deny the existence of any god.

My servants see those who pause to stop and think,
>those who examine the possibility of the error of their stance,
>those who readily accept the reality of a new truth now laid before
>>their eyes."

Eze 27:36 The merchants among the peoples will hiss at you; You will become a horror, and *be* no more forever.' " ' "
Divine Commentary—

"My servants beckon and encourage,
>gather some for prayer,
>gather some to witness the works of God,
>gather some to experience the works of God.

My servants put on offer the abilities of God to interact with man.

My servants rejoice with gladness at the upholding of His Word before the face of man."

My Content Study Aid

Divine Commentary— Ezekiel Ch 28

Eze 28:1 The word of the LORD came to me again, saying,
Divine Commentary—

"My servants mix with the proud and the vain,
        with all aspects of the character of man,
        with all aspects which bring him honouring by God,
        with all aspects which bring him respect by God,
        with all aspects which bring him to kneel before man,
        with all aspects which bring him the shame of man.

My servants mix and congregate within The Multitudes of man,
        within the nations,
        within the peoples,
        within the tongues,
                of man.

My servants preach and teach what does not leach;
    walk and talk but do not caulk;
    need and heed yet still do read:
            the word of God."

My Content Study Aid

Divine Commentary— Ezekiel Ch 29

Eze 29:1 In the tenth year, in the tenth *month,* on the twelfth *day* of the month, the word of the LORD came to me, saying,
Divine Commentary—

"My servants know the time of man,
    measure it with accuracy,
        watch it pass with the apparent movement of the sun,
            with the apparent movement of the heavens.

My servants watch the passing of time in the reflection of a face,
        in the restraints incurred upon a body,
        in the presentation of a flower upon the tree
            of life."

Eze 29:2 "Son of man, set your face against Pharaoh king of Egypt, and prophesy against him, and against all Egypt.
Divine Commentary—

"My servants change their status within the time of man,
    their family connections within the time of man,
    their happiness and grief within the time of man.

My servants change both their nature and their nurture in preparation for their walk
        with God."

Eze 29:3 "Speak, and say, 'Thus says the Lord GOD: "Behold, I *am* against you, O Pharaoh king of Egypt, O great monster who lies in the midst of his rivers, Who has said, 'My River *is* my own; I have made *it* for myself.'
Divine Commentary—

"My servants follow the leading of their God:
    commit to His antipathies,
    welcome that which He provides for the benefit of man."

Eze 29:4 But I will put hooks in your jaws, And cause the fish of your rivers to stick to your scales; I will bring you up out of the midst of your rivers, And all the fish in your rivers will stick to your scales.
Divine Commentary—

"My servants encounter the dispossessed:
    the damaged and deranged,
    the distraught and depressed,
    the devious and disgusting.

My servants encounter the developing:
    the delightful and dependable,
    the dancers and discerners,

> the discrete and the devout.

My servants know how they came to be as they are encountered.

My servants know of the curse of deprivation,
> know the blessing of the day.

My servants know the binding and the loosing—
> to demolish the cursing of the foe of man.

My servants know the keys of the Kingdom—
> to dictate a blessing on a life which has forsworn the idols
>> of generations.

My servants decrease the lost to Satan,
> increase the flock of The Good Shepherd."

My Content Study Aid

Divine Commentary— Ezekiel Ch 30

Eze 30:1 The word of the LORD came to me again, saying,
Divine Commentary—

"My servants feed upon My word,
 browse until they are content,
 savour and digest that which they have taken in.

My servants feed within their collective will where My word is to the fore,
 where My word is not adulterated,
 where My word has not been washed to fade
  the meaning and intent,
 where My word has not been washed solely
  for a claim of ownership,
 where My word has not been washed under
  a scrutiny of soapsuds which
  have not been rinsed away,
 where My word has neither been tailored to
  fit into a straitjacket nor left
  sprawling as the mess of man:
   yet still claimed to be divine.

My servants know those who cause My word to fail,
 who write to confuse the lost,
 who write to bend My word to fit their doctrines of the day,
 who write to comfort the misled and the miserable with
  doctrines not of God.

My servants know those who count the tithe of God for the benefit of men.

My servants know those who preach in hypocrisy,
 who preach new laws to their liking,
 who condone the uniting of sin with sin,
 who approve the preacher with the sin full soul from a bed
  of sin,
 who broadcast the lies of Satan,
  as modified for the correctness of the day,
  as being the untrammelled word of God."

My Content Study Aid

_____
_____

Divine Commentary— Ezekiel Ch 31

Eze 31:1 Now it came to pass in the eleventh year, in the third *month,* on the first *day* of the month, *that* the word of the LORD came to me, saying,
Divine Commentary—

"My servants active in their taskings inspire one another,
        like to exchange their stories,
        love to honour God.

My servants in among the souls of allocation are a joy to watch,
        besmearing the eyes of angels with some tears,
        besmearing the eyes of man with the tears of My Spirit,
            transforming a face into a radiance which speaks
                of divine attention,
                of experiencing the promises of God,
                of receiving first-hand—
                    knowledge of the reality of God."

Eze 31:2 "Son of man, say to Pharaoh king of Egypt and to his multitude: 'Whom are you like in your greatness?
Divine Commentary—

"My servants who share in anticipation are never disappointed,
        always catch the gleam of My Spirit,
        always reach out in love,
            in awareness of the enormity of the implication:
                for a successful ending of a task.

My servants sometimes have an insight into what they have been and done,
        into the meaning,
           the results,
              within the concept of eternity,
              within the fellowship of life,
                embedded in an ark they have
                    helped construct,
                set afloat with rejoicing souls,
                each on the adventure of a life—
                which no longer has an end."

Eze 31:3 Indeed Assyria *was* a cedar in Lebanon, With fine branches that shaded the forest, And of high stature; And its top was among the thick boughs.
Divine Commentary—

"My servants serve the arks of God,
        established and set free,
        refurnished and restored,

> replenished and revitalised,
> renewed and refreshed.

My servants love to encounter the flood tides of My Spirit,
> the flood tides of the harvest,
> the flood tides born through dependancy on preparation,
> > through thoroughness of homework,
> > through application of the will,
> > through practice of the tongues,
> > through focus on intent.

My servants are in wonder at the ebb and flow,
> as the flood tide deposits and uplifts,
> > baptises and releases into My Spirit's love—
> > > the timid and the tearful,
> > > the frightened and forlorn,
> > > the committed and the careful:
> > > those who would seek a new beginning for
> > > their lives under a change of heart.

My servants know the flood tides of My Spirit which carry My arks each to a birthplace:
> which is high and dry yet watered by
> > My Spirit,
> which is foreshadowed by My Spirit,
> which is a site preserved for presentation."

Eze 31:4 The waters made it grow; Underground waters gave it height, With their rivers running around the place where it was planted, And sent out rivulets to all the trees of the field.

Divine Commentary—

"My servants dwell within the watering of My Spirit,
> dwell within the showers of blessings,
> dwell within My Spirit's reign.

My servants bathe in the rivers of new life,
> drink from the cup which quenches thirst,
> submerge to arise under the hovering dove of God."

Eze 31:5 Therefore its height was exalted above all the trees of the field; Its boughs were multiplied, And its branches became long because of the abundance of water, As it sent them out.

Divine Commentary—

"My servants walk the road which leads each to their destiny,
> stop to rest at each way station,
> start again their journey eager for all the day brings forth,
> > eager to fulfill The Will of God,
> > eager to experience the satisfaction of their spirit

and their soul.

My servants walk in firmness of approach,
> in firmness of a welcome,
>> in firmness of the greeting of the day."

Eze 31:6 All the birds of the heavens made their nests in its boughs; Under its branches all the beasts of the field brought forth their young; And in its shadow all great nations made their home.
Divine Commentary—

"My servants stoop to conquer at the level of a child.

My servants stoop to conquer at the bedside of the elderly.

My servants stoop to conquer before a face in anguish at their feet.

My servants stoop to conquer illness in the wizened,
> the bent and the deformed.

My servants stoop to conquer the loss of height,
> the loss of standing,
> the disparity in height—
>> which puts one above another."

Eze 31:7 'Thus it was beautiful in greatness and in the length of its branches, Because its roots reached to abundant waters.
Divine Commentary—

"My servants do not shudder in revulsion,
> do not turn from a face brought for repair,
> do neither cringe before a temple in the making nor a temple of
>> The Living God.

My servants pray for all who present before them:
> that each may receive their crown of life—
>> of honour,
>> of the rejoicing of a spirit,
>> of the influx of My Spirit,
>> of the attentiveness of a soul."

Eze 31:8 The cedars in the garden of God could not hide it; The fir trees were not like its boughs, And the chestnut trees were not like its branches; No tree in the garden of God was like it in beauty.
Divine Commentary—

"My servants are attentive to The Faith expressed,
> to the needs made known,
> to the cure applied.

My servants know when to counsel,
> when to request compliance,

> when to make known The Will of God declared.

My servants know the delight of silence,
> know when to leave the rest to God,
> know when to release and so move on."

My Content Study Aid

Divine Commentary— Ezekiel Ch 32

Eze 32:1 And it came to pass in the twelfth year, in the twelfth *month*, on the first *day* of the month, *that* the word of the LORD came to me, saying,
Divine Commentary—
"My servants serve both God and man,
        serve God at His pleasure,
        serve man under direction.

My servants serve God within the bounds of fear,
        serve man within the bounds of respect for the mantles both carried
                          and encountered.

My servants serve their loving God within His covenant and their confession of joint
                              solidarity in love.

My servants serve man under the auspices of God,
        as disciples of God,
        as viceroys of God,
        as royal households in their realms adopted into The Family
                                  of God."

Eze 32:2 "Son of man, take up a lamentation for Pharaoh king of Egypt, and say to him: 'You are like a young lion among the nations, And you *are* like a monster in the seas, Bursting forth in your rivers, Troubling the waters with your feet, And fouling their rivers.'
Divine Commentary—
"My servants whether in their youth or whether in their maturity
                      have consistency of access,
                      have consistency of counsel,
                      have consistency within The Will of God.

My servants have consistency as their gifts expand with use,
        as their gifts develop with experience,
        as their gifts react as they are sought,
        as they are called to the fore,
        as they are shared as intended.

My servants do not shrug off the gifts of God,
        do not decline the gifts of God,
        do not deny the gifts of God.

My servants are not selective in a choice of gifts,
                in a rejection of some not to their liking,
                in an overuse of those with which they are familiar.

My servants,

in wisdom,
do not reject the gifts of God."

Eze 32:3 "Thus says the Lord GOD: 'I will therefore spread My net over you with a company of many people, And they will draw you up in My net.
Divine Commentary—

"The gifts of God are not repealed by God,
   are not cancelled by God,
   are not redeemed by God.

The gifts of God can not be pawned,
   should not be locked up in a vault,
   should not be kept in darkness far from the throne of light.

The gifts of God are for the discernment of My servant in his walk on The Earth,
   are for the protection of My servant in his venturing on The Earth,
   are for the ministering of My servant in the divine appointments
         encountered on The Earth.

The gifts of God are for the powerful and the humble,
   the rich and the poor,
   the lambs and the sheep.

The gifts of God grow in effectiveness with the growth in Faith,
   with the growth in tongues,
   with the growth in a relationship with God.

The gifts of God are as seeds planted in a garden where the soil is always fertile,
   which weeds cannot choke out,
   which may be dormant for
         a wintry season,
   which will grow to reach up to The Son
         light with tender loving care."

Eze 32:4 Then I will leave you on the land; I will cast you out on the open fields, And cause to settle on you all the birds of the heavens. And with you I will fill the beasts of the whole earth.
Divine Commentary—

"My servants should optimize their time within the age of Grace,
   optimize their preparation within the age of Grace,
   optimize their outreach for the lost within the age of Grace.

My servants should so structure all they say and do—
         in awareness of their presence within the age of Grace.

My servants need to broadcast to the world at large the significance of dwelling in the age of Grace.

My servants need to stress the benefits to the world at large—

of an understanding of all it means to man to be and live
within the age of Grace.

My servants need to ensure they are not held as accountable before a victim:
he who may accuse the knowledgeable yet silent,
he who may have walked and not been woken,
he who may have accompanied and yet not had shared,
he who has been subject to foreclosure of his time of Grace."

Eze 32:5 I will lay your flesh on the mountains, And fill the valleys with your carcass.
Divine Commentary—

"My servants are never seen by God as sacrificial lambs,
as lambs awaiting slaughter,
as lambs of little worth.

My earthbound servants have a special niche reserved within the hierarchy
of all who serve The God of Truth,
of all the hosts of Heaven,
of all who are self-aware,
of all who have been occasioned
with freewill.

My servants are always in the eye of God,
are as the cornerstone of His harvest,
are at the outworks of His Kingdom.

My servants are seen to be bound by their promises in validation of the word of God."

Eze 32:6 'I will also water the land with the flow of your blood, *Even* to the mountains; And the riverbeds will be full of you.
Divine Commentary—

"My servants are the viceroys of My Kingdom,
are the harbingers of hope,
are the settlors of confusion,
are the signposts for an eternal destiny,
are the brotherhood of God attending the brotherhood of man."

Eze 32:7 When *I* put out your light, I will cover the heavens, and make its stars dark; I will cover the sun with a cloud, And the moon shall not give her light.
Divine Commentary—

"My servants vie with others for the attention of the soul of man,
in order to change the outlook,
in order to offer Grace,
in order to ensure the sanctity of life,
in order to achieve all that which lies within The Will of God,
in order to extend a new covenant with man.

My servants have answers which unfold before the questioning of man,

> which enlist the counselling of My Spirit,
> which compromise demonic forces reliant on the idols
> > of deception,
> which shed The Light of truth upon the darkness of a lie,
> which entail the works of God before the eyes of man."

Eze 32:8 All the bright lights of the heavens I will make dark over you, And bring darkness upon your land,' Says the Lord GOD.
Divine Commentary—

"My servants enquire from the passers-by,
> explain their seeking of an answer,
> apologize for what is taken as an interruption,
> satisfy the seekers of further information.

My servants are as brushstrokes on a canvas:
> the brushstrokes of renewal which erase the darkness of the heart,
> the brushstrokes of an artist who can paint afresh,
> the brushstrokes which show great promise for a life revealed,
> the brushstrokes of the master in showing a life once restrained in
> > darkness uplifted to The Glory of The Light."

Eze 32:9 'I will also trouble the hearts of many peoples, when I bring your destruction among the nations, into the countries which you have not known.
Divine Commentary—

"My servants see the effects upon the canvas of a master painter,
> see the effects upon the clay of a master potter,
> see the effects upon a house of a master builder:
> > when destined to become a temple of The Living God.

My servants stand amazed before the work in progress,
> before the changes wrought,
> before the template of The Temple for the future life of man."

My Content Study Aid

_____
_____
_____
_____
_____
_____
_____

Divine Commentary— Ezekiel Ch 33

Eze 33:1 Again the word of the LORD came to me, saying,
Divine Commentary—

"My servants celebrate in jubilation at the outward evidence of their God at work within a life.

My servants have no constraint of the time of man in dealing to the devil,
        have no constraint of the time of man in the pursuit of freedom from satanic works,
        have no constraint of the time of man when about the works of God.

  For the works of God are not timetabled for the benefit of man,
        are not constrained by the bounds of time,
        are not turned off and on to satisfy a clock of man.

My servants should ensure by enquiry the completion of that which they have initiated
        in a child of God,
        in a sheep within a sheepfold,
        in a lamb in hands of loving care."

Eze 33:2 "Son of man, speak to the children of your people, and say to them: 'When I bring the sword upon a land, and the people of the land take a man from their territory and make him their watchman,
Divine Commentary—

"I,
  The Lord God of Abraham,
      say to My servants this day,
  'Let not the devil interrupt the ministry of God.

  Let not the usurper of salvation amass his forces at the outposts of My servants.

  Let not the devil rule through the ignorance of My servants.' "

Eze 33:3 'when he sees the sword coming upon the land, if he blows the trumpet and warns the people,
Divine Commentary—

"Again,
  I,
    The Lord Jesus,
      say this day to My servants,
        'Carry no fear for the devil.

      Carry no dismay upon your shoulders.

      Carry no disillusionment within your hearts.'

I,
> The Lord God,
>> in the presence of The Father,
>>> declare My servants are protected when walking in the boldness of their Faith,
>>>> in the boldness of My Spirit,
>>>> in the boldness due their
>>>>> ministry within
>>>>>> the arch of God."

Eze 33:4 'then whoever hears the sound of the trumpet and does not take warning, if the sword comes and takes him away, his blood shall be on his *own* head.
Divine Commentary—

"My servants all should know the power and the authority which backs the gift often
>> lying dormant within the mouth of every saint.

> For as the tongue of man can start a firestorm on The Earth,
>> so the tongues of My Spirit can start firestorms in the heavens,
>>> firestorms in the domain of Satan,
>>> firestorms throughout the totality of creation.

Wise are My servants who call the tongues of Heaven to confront satanic forces,
>>> to cause the likes to flee,
>>>> to bring to pass their absconding
>>>>> from the field of battle.

The purifying firestorms of God are the liquidators of the threat from satanic forces,
>>> set the bounds beyond which they cannot advance,
>>> hurl discordant forces into a mass retreat,
>>> subdue the activities of the foe of man."

Eze 33:5 'He heard the sound of the trumpet, but did not take warning; his blood shall be upon himself. But he who takes warning will save his life.
Divine Commentary—

"My servants do not clutch at the things of God,
>> do not secrete the gifts to avoid embarrassment,
>> do not hide The Glory of their gifts from the presence of man.

My servants were born to share:
>>> in this time with their callings,
>>> in this time of their taskings,
>>> in this time for their presences on The Earth.

My servants are not as shadows which come and go,
>> are not lightly dismissed from their tasks at hand,
>> are not overcome in the presence of The God of Love."

Eze 33:6 'But if the watchman sees the sword coming and does not blow the trumpet, and the people are not warned, and the sword comes and takes *any* person from among them, he is taken away in his iniquity; but his blood I will require at the watchman's hand.'

Divine Commentary—

"My servants serve in unity of purpose:
> can summon others to assist when outnumbered by the seekers,
>> when surrounded by the querulous,
>> when the spirit heeds the scent of victory.

My servants can accompany the rider on the white horse with a sign emblazoned on
>> his thigh,
>> as an arrow for a bow,
>> as a firebrand of attention,
>> as a burning arrow targeting
>>> a soul.

My servants are destined to overcome their opposition,
> to overcome the mischief of the day,
> to overcome the tempting of the night.

My servants overcome that which would forestall the works of God in the life of man."

My Content Study Aid

Divine Commentary— Ezekiel Ch 34

Eze 34:1 And the word of the LORD came to me, saying,
Divine Commentary—

"My servants have responsibilities attendant on their callings,
      attendant on the requirement to espouse the truth
            of God,
      attendant on their wisdom acquired since commencing
            their walk with God.

My servants have responsibilities ignored only by the fool.

My servants inherit responsibilities attendant on their confession of The Cross."

Eze 34:2 "Son of man, prophesy against the shepherds of Israel, prophesy and say to them, 'Thus says the Lord GOD to the shepherds: "Woe to the shepherds of Israel who feed themselves! Should not the shepherds feed the flocks?
Divine Commentary—

"My servants reach out for My staff of life,
    reach out for My bread and My wine,
    reach out for the companionship of God.

My servants are called to serve the word of God to the faces in a throng,
      to the faces in a crowd,
      to the faces called to gather within
          earshot of My servants.

My servants are to know the good news of My message,
      to expound the message of good news with clarity and love,
      to deliver forth in simplicity of speech without infringing the freewill of
          the gathered.

My servants are expected to be prepared to testify of their walk with God,
    are expected to encourage and uphold,
    are expected to be competent in leading lost souls in a confession of their
         new found Faith.

My servants serve no notice of apology for their aspects of delivery from the pulpit of
         The Lord.

The demeanour of My servants should carry The Fear of God."

Eze 34:3 "You eat the fat and clothe yourselves with the wool; you slaughter the fatlings, *but* you do not feed the flock.
Divine Commentary—

"My servants tend and assist,
    unyoke the yoked,

        unlock the locked,
        loose the bound,
        bind the loose.

My servants quench the thirst,
    feed the hungry,
        scatter the feeders on the carrion.

My servants supply the needs of widows,
    attend to the needs of orphans,
        take My message into rooms where the windows are all barred.

My servants know where My flock does feed,
    what My flock does need,
        why My flock does read."

Eze 34:4 "The weak you have not strengthened, nor have you healed those who were sick, nor bound up the broken, nor brought back what was driven away, nor sought what was lost; but with force and cruelty you have ruled them.
Divine Commentary—

"My servants who would shepherd the flock of God should know the order at a table,
        the order of a servant,
        the order which
            changes with the
            preference declared.

When order is seen as important so there is a shuffling in a queue,
    so there is activity by angels,
    so there is status evidenced before the eyes of man,
    so there is recompense on offer before the eyes of God.

My servants should not think the eyes of God can not see through a smokescreen
                                          of intent."

My Content Study Aid

_____

_____

_____

_____

_____

_____

_____

_____

Divine Intent— Ezekiel Ch 35

Scribal Note*: There are no specific divine commentaries on the content verses within this chapter.*

Upon enquiry of The Spirit as to the absence of such commentaries on Ezekiel Ch 35, The Lord shares His divine intent on this chapter:

"The words,
   I,
      The Lord,
         gave to My prophet Ezekiel still stand with relevance for these end-times—
               still stand as against the inhabitants of Mount Seir:
               still stand for the inhabitants of all the lands,
                     all the nations,
                     all the peoples,
                 all the tongues expressing hatred for
                         the land of Israel:
                 all not desiring peace;
                 all not dwelling in righteousness;
                 all who encompass war within
                         their hearts."

My Content Study Aid

_____
_____
_____
_____
_____
_____
_____
_____
_____
_____
_____
_____
_____
_____
_____

Divine Commentary— Ezekiel Ch 36

Eze 36:1 "And you, son of man, prophesy to the mountains of Israel, and say, 'O mountains of Israel, hear the word of the LORD!
Divine Commentary—

"My servants segregate the sacred from the profane.

My servants visit that for which they are tasked,
        that to which My Spirit guides,
        that in which is seen the handiwork of God.

My servants visit there to learn,
        visit there to teach,
        visit there for proclamation.

My servants visit there to pray,
        visit there to inspect,
        visit there to enthuse.

My servants visit the robed and the ragged,
        visit the draped and the dowdy,
        visit the formal and the frump,
        visit the costumed and the clothed,
        visit the bejewelled and the beggar,
        visit the suited and the shorts.

My servants visit at The Will of God.

My servants visit all the estates of man."

Eze 36:2 'Thus says the Lord GOD: "Because the enemy has said of you, 'Aha! The ancient heights have become our possession,' " '
Divine Commentary—

"My servants share all which they carry to the stopping points of God,
        all which is prepared as a sweet taste on the tongue,
        all which My Spirit provisions for delivery at a place and time.

My servants are examples of the gifts of My Spirit seen in action,
                in My ministry,
                in My blessings,
                in this age of Grace.

My servants are examples of My will deployed before the face of man.

My servants are examples of Faith triumphant on The Earth.

My servants are examples of applying the healing power of God,
        of moving in the authority of God,

of commanding and controlling the legions besetting man:
in the prayer releasing the healing love of God."

Eze 36:3 "therefore prophesy, and say, 'Thus says the Lord GOD: "Because they made *you* desolate and swallowed you up on every side, so that you became the possession of the rest of the nations, and you are taken up by the lips of talkers and slandered by the people"—
Divine Commentary—

"My servants are not intimidated by satanic forces,
> do not retreat,
> do not possess a flag which signifies surrender.

My servants understand the road to victory:
> which becomes littered with the enemy as each is cast aside
>> upon encounter.

My servants grapple and press the fall,
> do not withdraw until the victory ensures the shoulders flattened on the floor,
> do not relax until the foe scampers on his way,
> do not rejoice until the captive has the blessing of release,
>> until freedom is attained,
>> until My Spirit signs the conquest won.

My servants clash with the powers of darkness in the power of light.

My servants clash in anticipation of the severance of compatibility.

My servants clash in a class action against extreme malevolence,
> against extreme determination,
> against extreme commitment:
>> denying man his receiving of salvation under the canopy of Grace."

Eze 36:4 'therefore, O mountains of Israel, hear the word of the Lord GOD! Thus says the Lord GOD to the mountains, the hills, the rivers, the valleys, the desolate wastes, and the cities that have been forsaken, which became plunder and mockery to the rest of the nations all around—
Divine Commentary—

"My servants recognize disease which impacts on the body,
> which burrows from within,
> which is remorseless in attack on the flesh and bone.

My servants know the source of pain,
> know the source of sickness,
> know the source of ailments which beset the body.

My servants know to vaccinate the body so it can recover,
> to excise the seat of the infection,
> to clear the pathways of the plumbing,

    to clear the drains and wiring from blockages and static,
        from closed valves and short circuits,
        from the impeding of the watchmen
            stationed in the passages:
    to protect the occupants which dwell within the rooms.

My servants know the cleansing of the soul,
    the cleansing of the spirit,
    the scrubbing of the heart,
    the rinsing of the liver,
    the emptying of the stomach,
    the strengthening of supporting bones.

My servants are familiar with the components of a home,
    the structure of a house,
    The Glory of a temple:
      with their rooms intact."

Eze 36:5 'therefore thus says the Lord GOD: "Surely I have spoken in My burning jealousy against the rest of the nations and against all Edom, who gave My land to themselves as a possession, with wholehearted joy *and* spiteful minds, in order to plunder its open country." '
Divine Commentary—

"My servants see the devastation wrought on man by the plundering of Satan,
    see the cycles of despair:
    see the bowing to the idols which never answer man.

My servants see the gods of man silent throughout the centuries,
      bereft of comfort or of counsel,
      bereft of the reality of a godly impact on a life resulting
          from the devotions of man,
      bereft of the signature which signs a Living and
          a Loving God within the lives
          of those who know Him.

My servants see the gods born of idolatry which speak,
      in deception,
      the words of man:
        those then attributed to silent heaps of stone,
            of metal,
            of plastic,
            of gaudy
        paraphernalia not worth the offering
        tendered with a bowing head.

There,
  the words of man,

so instated,
curl the pages of the books claimed to be holy—
to be sacred—
to a cause long lost right from its derivation within the will of man.

For the will of man cannot bring forth The Will of God,
cannot declare The Will of God,
cannot proclaim The Will of God without severe contamination
from the arcane desires of man."

Eze 36:6 "Therefore prophesy concerning the land of Israel, and say to the mountains, the hills, the rivers, and the valleys, 'Thus says the Lord GOD: "Behold, I have spoken in My jealousy and My fury, because you have borne the shame of the nations."
Divine Commentary—

"My servants see the signs and wonders of their God in action,
see the miracles of healing which defy the reality of an explanation,
see the manifested results of prayer as offered up to their God,
see the manifested answers to prayer as rendered down to man,
see the gifts of My Spirit activated in each temple,
hear the tongues of angels on the tongue of man,
witness the healing of man in all its visitations,
in all its shapes,
in all its guises,
as evidenced in,
on,
as part of,
the being of man."

Eze 36:7 'Therefore thus says the Lord GOD: "I have raised My hand in an oath that surely the nations that *are* around you shall bear their own shame.
Divine Commentary—

"My servants endeavour not to walk the streets of shame alone,
endeavour not to put at risk that which they hold dear,
endeavour not to cross a street to look into a window of temptation,
endeavour not to seek that which they know they should not,
endeavour not to harm their ministry of partnership with God,
endeavour not to do the bidding of the devil."

Eze 36:8 "But you, O mountains of Israel, you shall shoot forth your branches and yield your fruit to My people Israel, for they are about to come.
Divine Commentary—

"My servants stand on the shoulders of those who have gone before.

My servants stand on the mountains of commitment raised up with great effort.

My servants stand upon the heights to look down upon the plains where there are the
dwelling of The Multitudes.

My servants stand to see the trees of righteousness growing bearing fruit.

My servants see the trees of righteousness planted,
>> watered,
>> pruned,
>> standing upright before a Loving God.

My servants stand to see the righteous forest spreading across the land."

Eze 36:9 "For indeed I *am* for you, and I will turn to you, and you shall be tilled and sown.
Divine Commentary—

"My servants receive the care,
> the attention,
>> of their Lord God.

My servants once were blind but now they see,
> once were dumb but now they speak,
> once were lost but now are found,
> once were fragments but now are whole,
> once were idle but now are tasked.

My servants know the birthing of new life in the soul,
> the bringing of new light upon the spirit,
> the presenting of the body,
>> the soul,
>> the spirit,
>> for the healing of all three."

Eze 36:10 "I will multiply men upon you, all the house of Israel, all of it; and the cities shall be inhabited and the ruins rebuilt.
Divine Commentary—

"My servants do not trample on the rice grains at home within the field,
> do not trample on the wheat grains at home upon the land,
> do not trample on the grains awaiting within the harvest due The Son.

My servants do not cause the shedding of the grains prior to the gathering of The Lord."

Eze 36:11 "I will multiply upon you man and beast; and they shall increase and bear young; I will make you inhabited as in former times, and do better *for you* than at your beginnings. Then you shall know that I *am* the LORD.
Divine Commentary—

"My servants hearken to the murmur of assent,
> hearken to the timid voice speaking in response,
> hearken to the questioning of the heart as to what the future holds.

My servants answer the call of man with wisdom and with understanding in the presence
>> of their God."

Eze 36:12 "Yes, I will cause men to walk on you, My people Israel; they shall take possession of you, and you shall be their inheritance; no more shall you bereave them *of children*."
Divine Commentary—

"My servants seek the spiritual of God,
>   seek the physical of man.

My servants would encourage the physicality of man to adopt the spirituality of God.

My servants declare in wisdom:
>   the extent of time within the physicality of The Earth,
>   the control of time within the spirituality of the realms of God.

My servants introduce those who seek from the limitations of the physical into the
>   unbounded possibilities of all within the spiritual.

My servants seek to usher all from the bounds of darkness into the realms of light.

My servants know the call of God upon their lives and their journeys home."

Eze 36:13 'Thus says the Lord GOD: "Because they say to you, 'You devour men and bereave your nation *of children*,'
Divine Commentary—

"My servants would that none should pass them by,
>   would that none should shake their heads,
>   would that none should turn away,
>   would that none should refuse a journey built on Grace,
>   would that all which is on offer be fully understood while it is today."

My Content Study Aid

Divine Commentary— Ezekiel Ch 37

Eze 37:1 The hand of the LORD came upon me and brought me out in the Spirit of the LORD, and set me down in the midst of the valley; and it *was* full of bones.
Divine Commentary—

"My servants encounter the challenges of God,
  encounter the testing of their Faith,
  encounter surprise at the tasks before them.

My servants see the visions laid before their eyes.

My servants see the visions in progression.

My servants see that which God intends.

My servants see the visions bringing understanding of the messages of God."

Eze 37:2 Then He caused me to pass by them all around, and behold, *there were* very many in the open valley; and indeed *they were* very dry.
Divine Commentary—

"My servants see the details with the scope,
  see the extent with the limits,
  see the content with the type.

My servants see that which is imprinted on the memory,
  declared unto the spirit,
  registered by the soul."

Eze 37:3 And He said to me, "Son of man, can these bones live?" So I answered, "O Lord GOD, You know."
Divine Commentary—

"My servants hear the soundtrack of the vision which holds the voice of God.

My servants respond within the wisdom of the moment.

My servants,
  in fear,
  are called to participate in a dialogue with God."

Eze 37:4 Again He said to me, "Prophesy to these bones, and say to them, 'O dry bones, hear the word of the LORD!
Divine Commentary—

"My servants in dialogue with God speak in fear born of their position,
  act in fear born of their understanding,
  serve in fear born of clean hands for the task,
  share in fear born as authority is granted."

Eze 37:5 'Thus says the Lord GOD to these bones: "Surely I will cause breath to enter

into you, and you shall live.
Divine Commentary—

"My servants in dialogue with God hear The Will of God declared as transfers of intent,
        hear the affirmations of His mouth,
            hear the dictates spoken for the records to be laid
                  before the eyes of man."

Eze 37:6 "I will put sinews on you and bring flesh upon you, cover you with skin and put breath in you; and you shall live. Then you shall know that I *am* the LORD." ' "
Divine Commentary—

"My servants tend The Will of God with alacrity,
    with clarity of purpose,
    with integrity in understanding,
    with wisdom as imparted.

My servants do not sit on a seesaw when in a dialogue with God,
    do not sit on a swing when in a dialogue with God,
    do not jump up and down when in a dialogue with God,
    do not skip a rope when in a dialogue with God.

My servants stand as if on a rock when in a dialogue with God."

Eze 37:7 So I prophesied as I was commanded; and as I prophesied, there was a noise, and suddenly a rattling; and the bones came together, bone to bone.
Divine Commentary—

"My servants see the fruits of their obedience born of The Fear arising from the presence
                  of their God.

My servants rejoice at their participation under The Fear of God.

My servants seek the comfort of relationships of honour with their loving God.

My servants hear their names when called,
    respond as willing servants,
    abide in the word of God."

My Content Study Aid

_____
_____
_____
_____
_____
_____

Divine Commentary— Ezekiel Ch 38

Eze 38:1 Now the word of the LORD came to me, saying,
Divine Commentary—

"My servants are expected to take into the temporal world of man that which they receive
from the spiritual dimensions of God.

My servants are expected to extend The Will of God.

My servants are endowed to fulfill The Will of God.

My servants are blessed to take the forts of Satan,
to prise out the shadowers in the darkness,
to set up the searchlights which therein highlight the souls
in bondage."

Eze 38:2 "Son of man, set your face against Gog, of the land of Magog, the prince of Rosh, Meshech, and Tubal, and prophesy against him,
Divine Commentary—

"My servants address the content of a fort,
the health of a fort,
the appearance of a fort.

My servants start the process of conversion to a temple,
start the process by declaring a higher road,
by declaring a better destination,
by declaring the companionship found along the way.

My servants pray My Spirit to sprout the seed of Faith,
to open ears so they may hear,
to open the spirit and the soul in unison within a
higher purpose,
to open the telescope of the fort to focus on The God
of Love."

Eze 38:3 "and say, 'Thus says the Lord GOD: "Behold, I *am* against you, O Gog, the prince of Rosh, Meshech, and Tubal.
Divine Commentary—

"My servants receive the words of knowledge to dumbfound the forts,
to restrict their angles of fire,
to concentrate the effort on the threshold of
the fort.

My servants besiege a fort with a weapon not often used in context,
not known to have a bearing on
the circumstance,

not often seen before on the scene of battle.

My servants should use the ram of God to gain entrance across the threshold of
satanic forts,
to gain access to a challenge,
to gain a respite of relief when an embattled soul
enquires as to the terms of surrender.

My servants use the presence of the ram as the rallying cry which brings the storming of
the fort."

Eze 38:4 "I will turn you around, put hooks into your jaws, and lead you out, with all your army, horses, and horsemen, all splendidly clothed, a great company *with* bucklers and shields, all of them handling swords.
Divine Commentary—

"My servants carry hooks of which they know very little,
carry hooks fitted for the jaws,
carry hooks which silence the trumpet of the fort.

My servants can whisper the unfolding prayer of God:
in the absence of the sounding of a trumpet when a hook is placed.

My servants seek the sharpening of the hooks:
by the word of God declared unto His servants."

Eze 38:5 "Persia, Ethiopia, and Libya are with them, all of them *with* shield and helmet;
Divine Commentary—

"My servants would do well to remember,
to recall the effect upon,
the woman at the well who heard her past recounted to her ears from one
who stood before.

My servants,
as they would follow in My footsteps,
are also so to do,
empowered,
equipped;
each resplendent in their bearing as envoys of The Lord."

Eze 38:6 "Gomer and all its troops; the house of Togarmah *from* the far north and all its troops—many people *are* with you.
Divine Commentary—

"My servants are present at the gatherings,
are present at the assemblies,
are present at the markets of the day,
are present when selecting the provisioning of life.

My servants are not placed as in a sandy desert where only the oasis carries life."

Eze 38:7 "Prepare yourself and be ready, you and all your companies that are gathered about you; and be a guard for them.
Divine Commentary—

"My servants are fortified against the forts,
    are sustained with the requirements for a task,
    are equipped with wisdom for discretion,
    are upheld by the authority,
        with the oversight,
           of the leading of My Spirit."

My Content Study Aid

Divine Commentary— Ezekiel Ch 39

Eze 39:1 "And you, son of man, prophesy against Gog, and say, 'Thus says the Lord GOD: "Behold, I *am* against you, O Gog, the prince of Rosh, Meshech, and Tubal;
Divine Commentary—

"My servants are familiar with the horoscopes of man,
>are familiar with the search of man for patterns.

My servants know of those who lay the tarot card,
>those who create a séance,
>>those who create the visual with a story line which fritters away the time of man,
>>>those who seek every opportunity to dip into the pocket,
>>>>the wallet or the purse of man:
>>>>>of all who seek the triviality of a false story of a soul."

Eze 39:2 "and I will turn you around and lead you on, bringing you up from the far north, and bring you against the mountains of Israel.
Divine Commentary—

"My servants are familiar with those known for their spiels,
>are familiar with the deceptive nature of their fruit,
>are familiar with the end product of a lie.

My servants hear the knock which should bring dismissal,
>are aware of the false lines of enquiry,
>>of each agenda hidden for the moment which surfaces in time.

My servants will not find the humble heart in distractions such as these,
>where a promise holds no worth,
>>where a guarantee does not last past departure of the vocal."

Eze 39:3 "Then I will knock the bow out of your left hand, and cause the arrows to fall out of your right hand.
Divine Commentary—

"My servants can disarm those who carry evil to the forecourts of The Lord,
>those who would spread their evil influence within the sphere of man,
>>those who would seek to impinge on the sacred and the righteous,
>>>those who would encroach upon the life and livelihood of man.

My servants disarm the opposition by the word of God,
>by the blood of God,
>by the testimony of His servants."

Eze 39:4 "You shall fall upon the mountains of Israel, you and all your troops and the

peoples who *are* with you; I will give you to birds of prey of every sort and *to* the beasts of the field to be devoured.
Divine Commentary—

"My servants see and do that which is not open to The Multitudes,
> that which has no meaning within their level of understanding,
> that which lasts beyond the grave of man,
> that which requires familiarity with a kingdom's keys,
> that which builds without destruction on the landscape
>> of eternity."

Eze 39:5 "You shall fall on the open field; for I have spoken," says the Lord GOD.
Divine Commentary—

"My servants see the end from the beginning,
> see the fallen and the slain,
> see the dampness of the line which marks a new beginning for the
>> newly unencumbered.

My servants are extremely buoyant in the presence of success,
> in the presence of a promise which holds the future destiny of man,
> in the presence of their loving God seen to be still shepherding His flock."

Eze 39:6 "And I will send fire on Magog and on those who live in security in the coastlands. Then they shall know that I *am* the LORD.
Divine Commentary—

"My servants love the word of God,
> hear the word of God,
> believe the word of God,
> live the word of God,
> practise the word of God,
> bring the word of God,
> share the word of God.

My servants pray with fluency for the word of God to be actioned in the life of man."

My Content Study Aid

_____
_____
_____
_____
_____
_____
_____

Divine Commentary— Ezekiel Ch 40

Eze 40:1 In the twenty-fifth year of our captivity, at the beginning of the year, on the tenth *day* of the month, in the fourteenth year after the city was captured, on the very same day the hand of the LORD was upon me; and He took me there.
Divine Commentary—

"My servants are the visionaries of God.

My servants are the seekers of My favour.
My servants are the flexors of My body.
My servants are the rescuers of My souls.

My servants are the minders of My purse strings for this day upon The Earth."

Eze 40:2 In the visions of God He took me into the land of Israel and set me on a very high mountain; on it toward the south *was* something like the structure of a city.
Divine Commentary—

"My servants are the translators of My will on Earth.

My servants are to witness the binding of the three-fold components of man—
          of body,
            soul and spirit—
    as they meld into a new identity where everything is changed,
    as they meld into a new identity which wakens as from sleep
        into a brand new day,
    as they meld into a new identity where eternity is introduced;
    where time is but a construct without authority to govern."

Eze 40:3 He took me there, and behold, *there was* a man whose appearance *was* like the appearance of bronze. He had a line of flax and a measuring rod in his hand, and he stood in the gateway.
Divine Commentary—

"My servants are the instigators of My will on Earth.

My servants are the flow-cards of determination,
    are the flow-cards which sustain the building of a kingdom,
    are the flow-cards of supervision in the estate of man.

My servants are the flow-cards which accumulate and clear the obstructions to
        The Kingdom:
      that of freedom of access,
        freedom of worship,
    to and for the soul of man."

Eze 40:4 And the man said to me, "Son of man, look with your eyes and hear with your ears, and fix your mind on everything I show you; for you *were* brought here so that I

might show *them* to you. Declare to the house of Israel everything you see."
Divine Commentary—

"My servants read that they may learn the ways of God,
> practise and assimilate that they may be equipped,
> verify and test that they may not be misled.

My servants of the living God participate with and sustain the sheep who stay within the
> > sheepfold claimed by God."

Eze 40:5 Now there was a wall all around the outside of the temple. In the man's hand was a measuring rod six cubits *long, each being a* cubit and a handbreadth; and he measured the width of the wall structure, one rod; and the height, one rod.
Divine Commentary—

"My servants dispel and restore,
> measure and encourage,
> uplift and wash the soul—
> > all within the confines of their callings,
> > > the bounding of their tasks,
> > > the companionship with God.

My servants are not as surgeons charged to lance a wound which festers,
> charged to lance an open boil,
> charged to lance a pus-ball built up of unrepented
> > > matters of the soul.

My servants are charged to pray the word of wisdom,
> to pray the word of knowledge,
> to pray the counsel of My Spirit,
> > for and on the one with a suffering soul.

My servants are charged to fear the timetable of God within the mortality of man.

My servants are not charged to charge outside The Will of God."

Eze 40:6 Then he went to the gateway which faced east; and he went up its stairs and measured the threshold of the gateway, *which was* one rod wide, and the other threshold *was* one rod wide.
Divine Commentary—

"My servants contain their feelings,
> enlist help according to My Spirit's call.

My servants do not vanquish the unforgiving,
> neither downplay the desolate nor distraught.

My servants are cheery in their dispositions,
> are grateful for each happy heart encountered.

My servants offer thanks for the beauty of creation as it becomes endemic within their
> > spirits and their souls."

Eze 40:7 Each gate chamber *was* one rod long and one rod wide; between the gate chambers *was a space of* five cubits; and the threshold of the gateway by the vestibule of the inside gate *was* one rod.
Divine Commentary—

"My servants offer thanks at the beginning of the day,
    offer thanks at the passing of the day,
    offer thanks for all they have encountered on the journey of the day.

My servants apply themselves to the tasking of the day,
    apply themselves within The Will of God,
    apply themselves as My Spirit leads."

Eze 40:8 He also measured the vestibule of the inside gate, one rod.
Divine Commentary—

"My servants value the accuracy of God,
    the preciseness of God,
    the directness of God.

My servants value the perspective of God,
    The Wisdom of God,
    the oversight of God.

My servants value the resources of God."

Eze 40:9 Then he measured the vestibule of the gateway, eight cubits; and the gateposts, two cubits. The vestibule of the gate *was* on the inside.
Divine Commentary—

"My servants neither hinder nor delay the works of God.

My servants do not ignore,
    do not vacillate,
    do not procrastinate when attending the workplace of The Lord.

My servants value promptness in attending,
    do not mix with laggards,
    are not counselled by the derelict of spirit."

Eze 40:10 In the eastern gateway *were* three gate chambers on one side and three on the other; the three *were* all the same size; also the gateposts were of the same size on this side and that side.
Divine Commentary—

"My servants are sensitive to the needs of others,
    are enabled to separate the wants and likes from the desires of the heart,
    are enabled to support a kindred soul about to buckle under load,
    are enabled to speak the word of God for the lightening of the load."

Eze 40:11 He measured the width of the entrance to the gateway, ten cubits; *and* the length of the gate, thirteen cubits.

Divine Commentary—

"My servants recognize a servant on the rebound,
>a servant on recovery,
>a servant reinvigorated,
>a servant with the tongues,
>a servant reinstated,
>a servant now recuperated,
>a servant no longer treading water,
>a servant no longer with dulled eyes.

My servants greet with smiles of welcome a servant on a furlough:
>a furlough speaking of recognition of extended service filled with honour:
>>at the frontiers of The Kingdom."

Eze 40:12 *There was* a space in front of the gate chambers, one cubit *on this side* and one cubit on that side; the gate chambers *were* six cubits on this side and six cubits on that side.

Divine Commentary—

"My servants are to build The Kingdom,
>are to construct The Edifice of God.

My servants are to know the measure of success,
>are to know the measure of defeat.

My servants apply the measure of success to the works of God.

My servants apply the measure of defeat to the works of Satan.

My servants are exact in their measuring,
>are precise in their procuring,
>neither waste nor seek a surplus to requirements."

Eze 40:13 Then he measured the gateway from the roof of *one* gate chamber to the roof of the other; the width *was* twenty-five cubits, as door faces door.

Divine Commentary—

"My servants are aware of what they need to request for the measure of the day:
>the measure which determines the outcome of the objective of the day:
>>as it is requested for a site of light,
>>as it is demanded at a site of darkness.

My servants sort in preparation,
>pray in expectation,
>open or close the shutters of the windows of a soul,
>loose or bind the spiritual as it is encountered,
>end each day in satisfaction at the outcome of the effort under the hand
>>of God."

Eze 40:14 He measured the gateposts, sixty cubits high, and the court all around the

gateway *extended* to the gatepost.
Divine Commentary—

"My servants can know the measure of all who cross their paths,
                            the upright and the gracious,
                            the liar and the deceiver.

The measure of a man is continuously known to God,
                is continuously evaluated by God,
                is continuously recorded as his life proceeds."

Eze 40:15 *From* the front of the entrance gate to the front of the vestibule of the inner gate *was* fifty cubits.
Divine Commentary—

"My servants expect the monitoring of man by God should not come as a surprise to man.

  For as man monitors man so he is monitored by God.

  So man shall peruse the end result of the monitoring by God.

  So man shall abide by the verdict on a life.

  So man shall accept the sentence justified—
                        when accountability is to the fore."

Eze 40:16 *There were* beveled window *frames* in the gate chambers and in their intervening archways on the inside of the gateway all around, and likewise in the vestibules. *There were* windows all around on the inside. And on each gatepost *were* palm trees.
Divine Commentary—

"My servants are at the forefront of existence in their accompanying of God,
        are at the forefront of a series of transformations in their time
                                  within mortality,
        are at the finality of the curtain call which transforms from the grave,
        are at the threshold of the fulfilment of a promise built on Faith,
        are bespoken by God as measured for eternity."

Eze 40:17 Then he brought me into the outer court; and *there were* chambers and a pavement made all around the court; thirty chambers faced the pavement.
Divine Commentary—

"My servants have no need to wend their way,
        have no reason to hesitate at a signpost,
        have no reason to toss a coin at a turning point of life.

My servants know the way,
        know the stepping stones of God,
        know the staircase to the heavens,
        know The Light before their feet,
        know the counsel and the guidance of My Spirit."

Eze 40:18 The pavement was by the side of the gateways, corresponding to the length of the gateways; *this was* the lower pavement.
Divine Commentary—

"My servants know The King of kings,
        know My sacrifice,
        know abounding Grace,
        know My Good News for mankind,
        know the giftings of My Spirit.

The God of love does not leave His sheep to wander where they may,
                to wander in the darkness without a beacon,
                to wander in the fog without a call."

Eze 40:19 Then he measured the width from the front of the lower gateway to the front of the inner court exterior, one hundred cubits toward the east and the north.
Divine Commentary—

"My servants measure and are measured,
        perceive and discover,
        request and receive.

My servants have tools available for use,
        available for application,
        available from within the provisioning of God.

    The tools of God have no stress fractures,
            have no strain lines,
            have no staleness of selection.

    The tools of God are released to address a life,
            are released to modify intent,
            are released to preserve freewill,
            are released to assist His servants of the day,
            are released so a soul may come to know The God of Grace."

Eze 40:20 On the outer court was also a gateway facing north, and he measured its length and its width.
Divine Commentary—

"My servants honour The Holiness of God,
        are sensitive in The Fear of their approach,
        are willing to wait upon their God.

My servants do not apply the urgency of man to the affairs of God,
        do not apply the circumstances of man as if the circumstances of God,
        do not wait,
            with impatience,
            with a tapping foot,
            with frequent glances at a clock.

My servants know in wisdom the clock of man is not the clock of God."

Eze 40:21 Its gate chambers, three on this side and three on that side, its gateposts and its archways, had the same measurements as the first gate; its length *was* fifty cubits and its width twenty-five cubits.
Divine Commentary—

"My servants do not die before the throne of God.

My servants are not presented by the scruff of the neck.

My servants come in honour to receive their treasure from the storehouse of their God.

My servants are enrobed with the gowns of Heaven,
> are before all those who assisted in their journeys,
>> who brought the ministry of God,
>> who uplifted and protected,
>> who recorded and delivered,
>> who watched and applauded,
>> who rejoiced and danced at the selections of a soul.

My servants bring their measures into the presence of their God.

My servants are familiar with The Standards of their God.

Eze 40:22 Its windows and those of its archways, and also its palm trees, *had* the same measurements as the gateway facing east; it was ascended by seven steps, and its archway *was* in front of it.
Divine Commentary—

"My servants of devotion often are very similar in their measurements,
> often are very similar in aspects of their lives,
>> often are very similar in the priorities as set within their lives.

My servants of devotion do not quibble over standards afforded one another,
> do not inspect with a wary eye,
>> do not share in confidence that which they would not have
>>> others know.

My servants of devotion set high standards of behaviour in the living of their lives.

My servants of devotion have their souls in subjugation to their spirits,
> have their bodies in subjugation to their souls,
>> have their characters matured as adjuncts to their spirits."

Eze 40:23 A gate of the inner court was opposite the northern gateway, just as the eastern *gateway;* and he measured from gateway to gateway, one hundred cubits.
Divine Commentary—

"My servants encounter measurements as denote the lost,
> encounter measurements which support the upright,
>> encounter measurements which commit the bearers to a lean,

> which bring crinkles near the top,
> which cause fraying at the edges,
> which result in submission to the weathering
>> of man.

My servants encounter that where measurement is lost within a fallen crumpled heap,
>> still capable of movement."

Eze 40:24 After that he brought me toward the south, and there a gateway was facing south; and he measured its gateposts and archways according to these same measurements.

Divine Commentary—

"My servants hold dear the measurements imparted from The Standards of God.

> The standards of God set for the measuring of man,
>> set to withstand the ages,
>> set to be long remembered.

> The standards of God changed from under the law of must to The Grace of willingness,
>> changed from the law of sacrifice to the sacrifice of mercy,
>> changed from the law of the fallen to The Grace due
>>> the reconciled.

My servants hold dear the imprints of God on the history of man.
My servants hold dear the presence of The Holy Spirit upholding The Standards of God.
My servants hold dear within their hearts the love of God."

My Content Study Aid

Divine Commentary— Ezekiel Ch 41

Eze 41:1 Then he brought me into the sanctuary and measured the doorposts, six cubits wide on one side and six cubits wide on the other side—the width of the tabernacle.
Divine Commentary—

"My servants lead The Multitudes into a form of prayer,
>> into a form of recognition of the existence of God,
>> into a form of acceptance of a Living God,
>> into a form of the need for a call to preparation,
>> into a form of realization of a Loving God.

So are the people measured in their comprehension of the divinity of Christ."

Eze 41:2 The width of the entryway *was* ten cubits, and the side walls of the entrance *were* five cubits on this side and five cubits on the other side; and he measured its length, forty cubits, and its width, twenty cubits.
Divine Commentary—

"My servants read of Ezekiel's encounter with the measuring of God:
>> of the attention given to the structure,
>> to the materials of construction,
>> to the features for installation,
>> to the doors of entrance,
>> to the ways of exit,
>> to the gates of walls.

So I,
>> The Lord God of Abraham,
>>> ask My servants this day,
>>> 'If this is the due care and attention lavished on a receptacle of Holiness:
>>>> yet that which does not bleed—
>>>> then how much more does He now value,
>>>>> care for,
>>>>> attend to,
>>>> the transformation of the being of man:
>>>> into a temple of The Living God wherein dwells
>>>>> His Holy Spirit?'

My servants should comprehend in fullness that which they see bleeding
>> awaiting preparation—
>> The Receptacles of Holiness,
>>> in this age of Grace."

Eze 41:3 Also he went inside and measured the doorposts, two cubits; and the entrance, six cubits *high;* and the width of the entrance, seven cubits.
Divine Commentary—

"My servants should not go unprepared into the tasks of God;
>> should not be unduly sequestered in the halls of learning;
>>> should seek,
>>> should find,
>>> should don,
>>>> the covering of The Lord—
>>>> the mantle befitting of His service—
>>>>> The Guardian of Faith.

My servants should not wantonly delay the service of their God."

Eze 41:4   He measured the length, twenty cubits; and the width, twenty cubits, beyond the sanctuary; and he said to me, "This *is* the Most Holy *Place*."
Divine Commentary—

"My servants gravitate to where My Spirit is active before the eyes of man.

My servants are rebuked when not already at a centre of the reigning of My Spirit.

My servants are not charged to chase,
>> are endowed to bring;
> are not charged to seek,
>> are commissioned to use—
>>> thereby to display—
>> the gifts of God in the environment of man."

Eze 41:5   Next, he measured the wall of the temple, six cubits. The width of each side chamber all around the temple *was* four cubits on every side.
Divine Commentary—

"My servants do not lack self-confidence when moving in the boldness of My Spirit,
> do not lack The Faith of miracles when Faith filled by My Spirit,
> do not lack the words—
>> which break into a heart—
>>> when sheltered by the mantle of My Spirit.

My servants do not give just lip service to My Spirit,
> but should live and breathe My Spirit in their daily walk with God.

For then will My servants carry overflowing cups which splash the living water upon the
>>>> needful and the faithless."

Eze 41:6   The side chambers *were* in three stories, one above the other, thirty chambers in each story; they rested on ledges which *were* for the side chambers all around, that they might be supported, but not fastened to the wall of the temple.
Divine Commentary—

"My servants are proficient in the use of the keys which wake the heavens,
>> of the keys which command attention.

My servants are proficient in the raising of the dead.

My servants are proficient in the call of Faith which achieves the waking of the dead,
>> in the call of Faith within The Will of God,
>> in the call of Faith initiated for the honouring of God.

My servants,
> in the waking of the dead,
>> must evaluate surroundings,
>> must not commit to a sideshow for the faithless,
>> must request the leaving of the scene by those with paucity of Faith.

My servants,
> in the waking of the dead,
>> should commit according to My Spirit,
>> when Faith is fully to the fore in a heart filled with purity of intent.

For as the measure is,
> so the measure is employed.

For as My Spirit finds,
> so My Spirit does.

For as My will is known,
> so My will is present for My servants to enact."

Eze 41:7 As one went up from story to story, the side chambers became wider all around, because their supporting ledges in the wall of the temple ascended like steps; therefore the width of the structure increased as one went up *from* the lowest *story* to the highest by way of the middle one.
Divine Commentary—

"My servants should not play with that which they do not understand,
> should acquire the confidence of certainty,
> should seek counsel from the wise,
> should be worthy of the trust deployed upon a servant."

Eze 41:8 I also saw an elevation all around the temple; it was the foundation of the side chambers, a full rod, *that is,* six cubits *high*.
Divine Commentary—

"My servants vary in their relationships with their God,
> may still be immature in their dealing with the spiritual,
> may still be ill at ease with the rebuffing of the demons,
> may still be quite uncertain in coming before their God.

My servants may have the innocence of youth,
> the brashness of youth,
> the fidelity of youth,
> the enthusiasm of youth.

My servants know the youth or maturity of man is not a function of his years,

> is not a function of his education,
> is not a function of his role in life.

My servants know the youth or maturity of man is dependent on his walk with God:
> on his relationship with God;
> on the status of his spirit;
> on the controlling of his soul;
> on the confession of his day."

Eze 41:9 The thickness of the outer wall of the side chambers *was* five cubits, and so also the remaining terrace by the place of the side chambers of the temple.
Divine Commentary—

"My servants know the gratification of service well performed,
> know the outcroppings of great joy,
> know the cloud bursts of The Spirit,
> know the hearts of overflowing thankfulness.

My servants are the well-wishers of My Spirit,
> are the extenders of a friendship,
> are the confirmers at the outposts of a kingdom,
> are the spectacles of outreach,
> are the forerunners introducing the healing will of God.

My servants are scattered far and wide upon The Earth,
> are domiciled in their lands of birth,
> > in their lands of choice,
> > in their lands of tasking by The Lord.

My servants bear record of their lives of service to their God of love."

Eze 41:10 And between *it and* the *wall* chambers was a width of twenty cubits all around the temple on every side.
Divine Commentary—

"My servants frequent The Edifice of God,
> the structure and the ministry of God upon The Earth:
> > the ways,
> > the means,
> > the counsel,
> > the guidance—
> of the loving for the loved.

My servants recognize the aura of The Lord,
> the aura which surrounds His servants,
> the aura of compassion which always greets the lost,
> the aura of divinity bestowed upon the promise of salvation."

Eze 41:11 The doors of the side chambers opened on the terrace, one door toward the north and another toward the south; and the width of the terrace *was* five cubits all

around.
Divine Commentary—

"My servants present an offer of uniqueness,
>an offer straight from God,
>an offer filled with benefits,
>an offer open to an earthbound life,
>an offer complete with a covenant of Grace,
>an offer instated by The Cross at Calvary.

>An offer which has no equal on The Earth.

>An offer for a new beginning,
>an offer which erases sin,
>an offer of renewal,
>an offer with impact on eternity,
>an offer to travel to a destination accompanied by God.

My servants offer that which has God as its draughtsman,
>which has been lived by God,
>which has been sealed by God,
>which is upheld by God.

My servants hold on offer a contract from divinity for the honouring of the soul of man,
>a contract without peer,
>a contract based on love,
>a contract with The Living God,
>a contract for eternity—
>>the new covenant with God."

Eze 41:12 The building that faced the separating courtyard at its western end *was* seventy cubits wide; the wall of the building *was* five cubits thick all around, and its length ninety cubits.
Divine Commentary—

"My servants are enthralled by all which they are empowered to offer:
>>the incarnate life of Christ,
>>the tidings of good news,
>>the reconciliation of The Cross,
>>the defeating of the grave,
>>the invitation to join The Family of God,
>>the indwelling of The Holy Spirit,
>>the vanquishing of death,
>>the garden of serenity:
>>the roadmap to the stars."

Eze 41:13 So he measured the temple, one hundred cubits long; and the separating courtyard with the building and its walls *was* one hundred cubits long;
Divine Commentary—

"My servants have souls freed from imprisonment,
> have souls open to pursue the carriageway of God,
> have souls released from earthly temptations,
> have souls which learn to soar,
> have souls which rest on mountaintops to survey the views,
> have souls attended by bands of angels,
> have souls overseen by their spirits which rejoice.

My servants are in preparation for their planned return into the presence of their God."

Eze 41:14 also the width of the eastern face of the temple, including the separating courtyard, *was* one hundred cubits.
Divine Commentary—

"My servants awake with excitement to their tasks before them,
> to their tasks ordained at their prior creation in the presence of God,
> to the tasks ordained them for this very season of their time on Earth.

My servants know the sanctity of their callings,
> walk in the reality of their God,
> affirm the truthfulness of His witnesses who did not recant."

Eze 41:15 He measured the length of the building behind it, facing the separating courtyard, with its galleries on the one side and on the other side, one hundred cubits, as well as the inner temple and the porches of the court,
Divine Commentary—

"My servants awake with anticipation as they greet each day,
> as their tasks are laid before them,
> as they are equipped with understanding for all within this day.

My servants have variety in their tasks as the hands of God."

Eze 41:16 their doorposts and the beveled window frames. And the galleries all around their three stories opposite the threshold were panelled with wood from the ground to the windows—the windows were covered—
Divine Commentary—

"My servants see to the doctorings of God.

My servants see to the nursings of God.

My servants oversee the illness,
> oversee the recovery,
> oversee the re-instatement of a life.

My servants know the status of their servanthood,
> the value of their servanthood,

the need for their servanthood.

My servants remain unaware of the impact on eternity of their servanthood—
>> that which is tested to survive the grave;
>> that which contributes to the awaiting
>>> treasure chest stored for mortal man:
>> that which is withheld as a mystery of God."

Eze 41:17 from the space above the door, even to the inner room, as well as outside, and on every wall all around, inside and outside, by measure.
Divine Commentary—

"My servants vacate localities,
> landscapes,
> nations,
>> which deny a welcome,
> vacate where My Spirit gives no sign,
> vacate when discharged by the authority of man as he usurps the authority of God.

My servants do not vacate at the first request of man,
> do not vacate at the second ordering of man.

My servants vacate at the third instructing of man which writes in the record of dissent."

Eze 41:18 And *it was* made with cherubim and palm trees, a palm tree between cherub and cherub. *Each* cherub had two faces,
Divine Commentary—

"My servants walk in certainty of purpose within the idolatry of man,
> within The Will of God.

My servants cannot plead ignorance when they have not sought The Will of God.

My servants cannot plead disobedience as being within The Will of God.

My servants cannot plead connivance as being within The Will of God.

My servants cannot plead the greater good as being within The Will of God.

My servants should not plead the frivolous as being within The Will of God."

Eze 41:19 so that the face of a man *was* toward a palm tree on one side, and the face of a young lion toward a palm tree on the other side; thus *it was* made throughout the temple all around.
Divine Commentary—

"My servants are to know My Banner of declaration,
> My Flag of assembly,
> My Standard of possession.

My servants are to know the emblem of My Spirit which unites My people,
> the emblem of My Spirit which denotes My people,

> the emblem of My Spirit which signs to the lost.

> My servants are to witness the emblem of My Spirit which proscribes the works of Satan."

Eze 41:20 From the floor to the space above the door, and on the wall of the sanctuary, cherubim and palm trees *were* carved.
Divine Commentary—

> "My servants rejoice at the completed tasks of God,
>> at the fulfilment of the visions birthed within the heavens,
>> at the dissemination of the word of God throughout The Earth,
>> at The End-time release of The Holy Spirit's counselling of the servants of the living God,
> at the release of visions before the people within the enclaves of the lost."

Eze 41:21 The doorposts of the temple *were* square, *as was* the front of the sanctuary; their appearance was similar.
Divine Commentary—

> "My servants bring changes from the past of man into his present,
>> bring changes wrought through perseverance for the benefit of man,
>> bring changes at the behest of God into the fellowship of man."

Eze 41:22 The altar *was* of wood, three cubits high, and its length two cubits. Its corners, its length, and its sides *were* of wood; and he said to me, "This *is* the table that *is* before the LORD."
Divine Commentary—

> "My servants bring the offering laid upon a cross—
>> now the risen King of kings,
>> now The Christ with His mission seen in completion,
>> now The Christ who beckons one and all to accept the loving Grace-filled news."

Eze 41:23 The temple and the sanctuary had two doors.
Divine Commentary—

> "My servants tender the fare of God to complete the tables laid by man.

> The loving God invites man now to partake in the feast of kings."

My Content Study Aid

_____
_____
_____
_____

Divine Commentary— Ezekiel Ch 42

Eze 42:1 Then he brought me out into the outer court, by the way toward the north; and he brought me into the chamber which *was* opposite the separating courtyard, and which *was* opposite the building toward the north.
Divine Commentary—

"His servants come and go.

His servants bustle hustle jostle.

His servants take according to the size of pot.

His servants do not know the constraints of God,
        do not know My will,
        do not seek confirmation of My Spirit in advance."

Eze 42:2 Facing the length, *which was* one hundred cubits (the width was fifty cubits), was the north door.
Divine Commentary—

"His servants are self-named.

His servants carry sin in the absence of repentance,
        in the absence of impunity,
        in the face of the defiance of My word,
        in the face of the likely consequences.

His servants boast and count.

His servants listen and dismiss.

His servants gloat and scoff."

Eze 42:3 Opposite the inner court of twenty *cubits,* and opposite the pavement of the outer court, *was* gallery against gallery in three *stories*.
Divine Commentary—

"His servants are anathema to the flock of God.

His servants circle and separate,
        seize and keep,
        gnaw and incapacitate.

His servants scowl and control,
        argue and backbite,
        grab and store.

His servants bicker and dismay,
        influence and corrupt,
        chatter and reveal.

His servants entice and tempt,

> display and accompany,
> settle and mislead."

Eze 42:4 In front of the chambers, toward the inside, *was* a walk ten cubits wide, at a distance of one cubit; and their doors faced north.
Divine Commentary—

"His servants are the drivers of discord,
> are the smiters of the night,
> are the purveyors of the drivel,
> are the rustlers of the day.

His servants encamp within the bounds of Temples,
> within the bounds of man,
> within the milieux of the lost."

Eze 42:5 Now the upper chambers *were* shorter, because the galleries took away *space* from them more than from the lower and middle stories of the building.
Divine Commentary—

"His servants secrete and deposit,
> impart and surround,
> despise and linger.

His servants impose and entangle,
> delay and forestall,
> withdraw and regather.

His servants answer and confess,
> cheat and lie,
> assemble and attack."

Eze 42:6 For they *were* in three *stories* and did not have pillars like the pillars of the courts; therefore *the upper level* was shortened more than the lower and middle levels from the ground up.
Divine Commentary—

"His servants retreat and reassemble,
> appeal and admit,
> assess and initiate.

His servants report and administer,
> open and infect,
> trouble and influence.

His servants access and cling,
> install and impede,
> listen and block."

Eze 42:7 And a wall which *was* outside ran parallel to the chambers, at the front of the chambers, toward the outer court; its length *was* fifty cubits.

Divine Commentary—

"His servants are the objects of great evil,
    are the servants of the foe of man,
    are the breeders of confusion for the soul,
        of controversy for the spirit,
        of contagion for the body,
    are the contaminants of man.

His servants have a destiny reserved which is met with disbelief."

My Content Study Aid

Divine Commentary— Ezekiel Ch 43

Eze 43:1 Afterward he brought me to the gate, the gate that faces toward the east.
Divine Commentary—

"His servants are not concerned with the welfare of man,
    are concerned with nothing but the degradation of man.

His servants tempt with the despicable,
    lure within the licensing of lust,
    saturate the surroundings with sex,
    develop discourses of depravity,
    signal the signs of stupidity,
    rage through the reserves of the ragged.

His servants vest the vapours on the vacuous,
    dress the damsels in distress,
    yoke the youths to yield.

His servants impair the ability of man,
    the judgment of man,
    the character of man.

His servants instigate the inflicting of the incidents of idols on the life of man."

Eze 43:2 And behold, the glory of the God of Israel came from the way of the east. His voice *was* like the sound of many waters; and The Earth shone with His glory.
Divine Commentary—

"My servants carry and do not drop,
    support and sustain,
    vanquish and verify.

My servants uphold the rights of man,
    uphold the freewill of man,
    uphold the holding forth of Faith."

Eze 43:3 *It was* like the appearance of the vision which I saw—like the vision which I saw when I came to destroy the city. The visions *were* like the vision which I saw by the River Chebar; and I fell on my face.
Divine Commentary—

"His servants are the handicappers of man,
    are the destroyers of security,
    are the voyeurs of the soul.

His servants are the seekers of disaster,
    are the wreckers of a marriage,
    are the installers of the orphans."

Eze 43:4 And the glory of the LORD came into the temple by way of the gate which faces toward the east.
Divine Commentary—

"My servants repel the boarders.

My servants disentangle relationships.
My servants consolidate positions.
My servants practise righteousness.

My servants sear the wounds with My Spirit's torch."

Eze 43:5 The Spirit lifted me up and brought me into the inner court; and behold, the glory of the LORD filled the temple.
Divine Commentary—

"His servants blaspheme and curse,
            swear and victimize,
            segregate and mutilate.

His servants shout and scream,
            intimidate and assassinate,
            murder and manipulate."

Eze 43:6 Then I heard *Him* speaking to me from the temple, while a man stood beside me.
Divine Commentary—

"My servants are the watchmen on the watchtowers,
            are the guardians of the just,
            are the preservers of the morality of God.

My servants are the friends of God,
            are the speakers of the truth,
            are the carriers of the bread of life to a hungry world."

Eze 43:7 And He said to me, "Son of man, *this is* the place of My throne and the place of the soles of My feet, where I will dwell in the midst of the children of Israel forever. No more shall the house of Israel defile My holy name, they nor their kings, by their harlotry or with the carcasses of their kings on their high places.
Divine Commentary—

"The servants of The Earth comprise the good and the bad,
            the righteous and the wicked,
            the sacred and the evil.

The servants of The Earth protect or violate a trust,
            encourage or discourage a smile upon a face,
            remember or dismiss the veneration due The Saints of God."

Divine Commentary— Ezekiel Ch 44

Eze 44:1 Then He brought me back to the outer gate of the sanctuary which faces toward the east, but it *was* shut.
Divine Commentary—

"My servants dwell in the guidance of the most high God,
        in The Wisdom imparted from the most high God,
        in The Grace of blessings from the most high God,
        in the favour of relationship with the most high God.

My servants and their God in the relationship of love,
        with honour,
        with serving,
    should be the envy of the peoples,
        the nations of The Earth."

Eze 44:2 And the LORD said to me, "This gate shall be shut; it shall not be opened, and no man shall enter by it, because the LORD God of Israel has entered by it; therefore it shall be shut.
Divine Commentary—

"My servants have a record of developing the nations in which they dwell,
        in attaining the heights of achievement,
        in sharing the wealth of God in the
            communities in which they live,
        in uplifting the souls in deprivation into a
            new found freedom,
        in accommodating the orphans and the
            widows with the meeting of their needs."

Eze 44:3 "*As for* the prince, *because* he *is* the prince, he may sit in it to eat bread before the LORD; he shall enter by way of the vestibule of the gateway, and go out the same way."
Divine Commentary—

"My servants see what is before their eyes,
        that which has befallen them as blessings from their God—
            the blessing of the peoples,
            the blessing of the lands,
            the blessing of the nations as they grow
                and develop:
    each as from a baby in its infancy to a giant in its maturity."

Eze 44:4 Also He brought me by way of the north gate to the front of the temple; so I looked, and behold, the glory of the LORD filled the house of the LORD; and I fell on my face.

Divine Commentary—

"My servants see what is before their eyes,
>that which has befallen those as recompense for their Faith of failure—
>>the stagnation of the centuries in the lands of idolatry,
>>the stunting of the peoples of the idols,
>>the nations of the idle where the gods of stone,
>>>of resin,
>>>of clay,
>>>>say nothing,
>>>>do nothing,
>>as the growth in their surroundings does not surpass
>>>the introduction of new life."

Eze 44:5 And the LORD said to me, "Son of man, mark well, see with your eyes and hear with your ears, all that I say to you concerning all the ordinances of the house of the LORD and all its laws. Mark well who may enter the house and all who go out from the sanctuary.

Divine Commentary—

"My servants see the difference between the nations of outreach and the nations
>of recluse,
>between the lands taught to share and the lands who want
>>to keep,
>between the peoples with a vision and the peoples
>>without such to their name.

My servants see the difference between those who smile to light the way and those with
>downcast eyes who mumble in their beards.

My servants see the differences between the followers of The Loving God upon The
>Cross and the gods of multiplicity as idols with their hearts of stone."

Eze 44:6 "Now say to the rebellious, to the house of Israel, 'Thus says the Lord GOD: "O house of Israel, let Us have no more of all your abominations.

Divine Commentary—

"My servants see the effect wrought from a multiplicity of idols—
>the paraphernalia of the ministry of stone—
>the employer of the hierarchies of the priests of coloured dress.

The coloured dress donned to signify their standing before the eyes of man,
>to signify the beggars borne of idleness of purpose,
>to signify their attending the gods which never speak,
>>which never were,
>>which are not now,
>>which will never be."

Eze 44:7 "When you brought in foreigners, uncircumcised in heart and uncircumcised in flesh, to be in My sanctuary to defile it—My house—and when you offered My food,

the fat and the blood, then they broke My covenant because of all your abominations.
Divine Commentary—

"My servants see the make-believe priests of idols tending to their duties
        of polishing their stonework,
        of polishing their marble and their lacquers,
        of calling the ignorant of God to follow the stupidity of man,
                to bend the knee,
                to prostrate themselves,
                to make offerings,
                to attend the calls to prayer—
        yet never question why the blessings never flow.

My servants see the idol statues of the stonework glower down upon the peoples—
        with faces carved from the nightmares of the soul.

My servants see the peoples passing by,
    see the peoples making smoke of incense—
        for the dead nostrils of the stonework of man,
    see the effects of willing enslavement of the peoples—
        to the false religiosity of the priests garbed in their
            finery for the impressing of man."

Eze 44:8 "And you have not kept charge of My holy things, but you have set *others* to keep charge of My sanctuary for you."
Divine Commentary—

"My servants know The Wisdom of God far exceeds the wisdom of man;
        whether man is stuck in meditation,
        or bound within the books—
            those which claim,
            but cannot bring,
            enlightenment:
        either to the spirit or the soul of man."

Eze 44:9 Thus says the Lord GOD: "No foreigner, uncircumcised in heart or uncircumcised in flesh, shall enter My sanctuary, including any foreigner who *is* among the children of Israel.
Divine Commentary—

"My servants know,
    through first-hand experience,
    the answer to the quandary of the peoples with false gods—
        all those they cannot ever know,
        all those instated by man for the benefit of the so-called priests—
            the payers of homage to such before the peoples,
                on the lands,
                in the nations.

The so-called priests are stuck in a time warp of misplaced belief while calling on the
multitudes to support their chicanery—
the peoples whom they do not honour,
but rob of opportunity of advancement.

For the so-called priests suffocate the freewill of man as they favour a
non-existent Faith,
as they fail the test of truth,
as they deny the living God
everywhere abounding
in uniqueness."

Eze 44:10 "And the Levites who went far from Me, when Israel went astray, who strayed away from Me after their idols, they shall bear their iniquity.
Divine Commentary—

"My servants know to test the spirit of those who profess intimacy of relationship
with God,
to discard the false,
to expose the con men of religion,
to deny the idolaters who find begging quite acceptable,
who do not fear their gods,
who do not fear The Living God."

Eze 44:11 "Yet they shall be ministers in My sanctuary, *as* gatekeepers of the house and ministers of the house; they shall slay the burnt offering and the sacrifice for the people, and they shall stand before them to minister to them.
Divine Commentary—

"My servants do not shy from that which carries the imprint of the devil,
which carries the signature of Satan,
which carries the falsehoods of the ages,
which attempts to negate the truth of
The Cross of Christ,
the grave of Christ,
the seating of Christ."

Eze 44:12 "Because they ministered to them before their idols and caused the house of Israel to fall into iniquity, therefore I have raised My hand in an oath against them," says the Lord GOD, "that they shall bear their iniquity.
Divine Commentary—

"My servants know that which is declared,
that which is expected,
that which does not call for shame.

My servants know the past,
know the present,
have access to the future of man within The Will of God.

My servants know of the coming judgment of God upon The Multitudes,
> of the coming storm of tribulation,
>> of the need for preparation of all who would be counted within The
>>> Bride of Christ."

Eze 44:13 "And they shall not come near Me to minister to Me as priest, nor come near any of My holy things, nor into the Most Holy *Place;* but they shall bear their shame and their abominations which they have committed.
Divine Commentary—

"My servants can improve their relationships with God,
> can improve their devotion to a calling,
> can improve their response to God.

My servants should not avoid the obvious,
> should not delay the necessary,
> should not overlook their tribute to The King."

Eze 44:14 "Nevertheless I will make them keep charge of the temple, for all its work, and for all that has to be done in it.
Divine Commentary—

"My servants would do well to emulate the servant who found it necessary
> to come before My prophet John,
> to kneel before My prophet John,
> to be baptized in the fulfilment of all righteousness.

My servants sometimes do not practice what they preach—
> are thereby candidates for a title they may not like,
>> yet which is true,
>> which is deserved,
>> which is verified by the record of the body:
> that which impinges as a missing component on the walk with God."

Eze 44:15 "But the priests, the Levites, the sons of Zadok, who kept charge of My sanctuary when the children of Israel went astray from Me, they shall come near Me to minister to Me; and they shall stand before Me to offer to Me the fat and the blood," says the Lord GOD.
Divine Commentary—

"My servants should acknowledge the necessity for the composites of Faith.

So that Faith may be unimpaired.

So that Faith may continue to grow.

So that Faith may not be stunted by a road block.

So that Faith may be able to lead in the exaltation of man.

My servants should be fully saturated in removing the shadows of the past,
> should be set free to enjoy their time with God,

should not bear the weight of a stained soul in a daily walk."

Eze 44:16 "They shall enter My sanctuary, and they shall come near My table to minister to Me, and they shall keep My charge.
Divine Commentary—

"My servants look on the varied landscapes of The Earth and marvel at the handiwork
of God;
    look on the seas of splendour—
        the venues of life in great abundance—
            and are amazed at the foresight of God;
    look on the resources in The Earth and are silenced by the intent of God.

My servants would show wisdom in not permitting the season of the intellect of the
    scientist to dislodge the inheritance of wonderment set before a child.

My servants who have their doubts of Faith need to look more closely at the imprinted
    stamp of God:
        on the inherent miracles of God within a single cell of life."

Eze 44:17 "And it shall be, whenever they enter the gates of the inner court, that they shall put on linen garments; no wool shall come upon them while they minister within the gates of the inner court or within the house.
Divine Commentary—

"My servants should not give credence to the prying and the peering of man in his towers
    of learning,
        to his assertion life can arise from a hodgepodge
            of a soup,
        to his assertion life has a spontaneous act of
            coming instantly into existence,
        to his assertion that that which is now not now is:
            with the ability to replicate.

The stupidity of man does not do him credit,
    does not say anything for the training of his intellect,
    does not say anything in support of his supposed common sense."

Eze 44:18 "They shall have linen turbans on their heads and linen trousers on their bodies; they shall not clothe themselves with *anything that causes* sweat.
Divine Commentary—

"My servants should determine the reasoning as to why the pokers and the prodders
    gather round that which already carries life:
        with the information so arranged for manipulation
            of the most extreme complexity—
        within the ultimate in simplicity of design.

My servants rightly suspect the pokers and the prodders work to sustain a theory:
    even to the exclusion of the facts openly before them."

Eze 44:19 "When they go out to the outer court, to the outer court to the people, they shall take off their garments in which they have ministered, leave them in the holy chambers, and put on other garments; and in their holy garments they shall not sanctify the people.
Divine Commentary—

"My servants seek and respond to questioning on their God,
        to justify their Faith,
        to share their testimonies of God within their lives."

Eze 44:20 "They shall neither shave their heads nor let their hair grow long, but they shall keep their hair well trimmed.
Divine Commentary—

"My servants are the segments of the whole,
    are the supporters of the holy,
    are the repositories of knowledge,
    are the results of the ministry of God,
    are the evidence of things unseen impacting on the seen,
    are the agents of the gifts of God."

Eze 44:21 "No priest shall drink wine when he enters the inner court.
Divine Commentary—

"My servants do not venture into the realm of make-believe,
        into the realm of fantasy,
        into the realm of fiction,
        into the realm of cults where the agency of man—
                the freewill of man—
                has been surrendered without recourse."

Eze 44:22 "They shall not take as wife a widow or a divorced woman, but take virgins of the descendants of the house of Israel, or widows of priests.
Divine Commentary—

"My servants are The Temples of My Spirit,
    are the torches for My Spirit's flame,
    are the reservoirs which contain the living water.

My servants know the server of the ace of God—
        immune from interference.

My servants recognize the ace of God which silences the opposition,
        which never is returned,
        which always hits the targets of the day."

Eze 44:23 "And they shall teach My people *the difference* between the holy and the unholy, and cause them to discern between the unclean and the clean.
Divine Commentary—

"My servants know the fiery arrow sent to a seeking heart,

> to a troubled heart,
> to a heart in need,
> to a heart calling out for help.

My servants should always be prepared to attend promptly to the given task at hand."

Eze 44:24 "In controversy they shall stand as judges, *and* judge it according to My judgments. They shall keep My laws and My statutes in all My appointed meetings, and they shall hallow My Sabbaths.
Divine Commentary—

"My servants value highly their time with God,
> do not keep Him in a shoebox to be opened at their convenience,
> do not delay on seeking the message of the day,
> do not frown upon a tasking set by God.

My servants are a joy to behold when occupied by God,
> are a joy to visit when acting on behalf of God,
> are a joy to encounter when about the works of God.

My servants are to the fore in blessings when in the service of their God."

My Content Study Aid

Divine Commentary— Ezekiel Ch 45

Eze 45:1 "Moreover, when you divide the land by lot into inheritance, you shall set apart a district for the LORD, a holy section of the land; its length *shall be* twenty-five thousand *cubits,* and the width ten thousand. It *shall be* holy throughout its territory all around.
Divine Commentary—

"My servants keep sacred the things of God,
>> protect them from the profane,
>> uphold them before God.

My servants with souls of light may come before My altar,
>> may attend the preparation with the serving,
>>> of all which is done in My remembrance by The Saints of God.

My servants have no shelter in their sin before the sacrament of God.

My servants have no covering of life if they bring profanity to My cup when raised to
>> their lips.

My servants focus contamination on their mouth when placing the bread of life into a
>> cavern of disgust.

My servants often skip over My words requiring purity before the table of The Lord."

Eze 45:2 "Of this there shall be a square plot for the sanctuary, five hundred by five hundred *rods,* with fifty cubits around it for an open space.
Divine Commentary—

"My servants,
> in wisdom,
>> should confess in love and affirmation when in possession of a repentant heart.

My servants can stall their progress with their God without having the assurance of
>> My Spirit:
>>> as they come before the throne of God.

My servants must not become complacent in their observance of My sacrament
>> of honour:
>>> where they become forgetful of My Grace.

For as each appears before The Altar of The Lamb:
>> so he will be accepted or rejected—
>> for his level of preparation for The Bride.

For this is the time for the preparation of My servants:
>> wise are they who attend to the changes needed:
>> for the purity of My Bride.

For as each partakes of My sacrament so the bells of angels toll:
> in the love time of My blessings;
> in the panic of alarm.

So the record stands until the call for Grace descends:
> both to forgive and to erase.

My servants are ill-advised not to guard their souls while it is today."

Eze 45:3 "So this is the district you shall measure: twenty-five thousand *cubits* long and ten thousand wide; in it shall be the sanctuary, the Most Holy *Place*.
Divine Commentary—

"My servants are rebuked when they are in danger of breaching
> what is acceptable before The Lord,
> what is acceptable in their daily lives,
> what is acceptable in their walk with God.

My servants sometimes need the rebuke of love as they are seen to walk in peril:
> close to the edges of the straight and narrow way.

My servants are rebuked for walking along the edges of the cliff tops:
> without the security of a net.

My servants are rebuked for needlessly putting their lives at risk:
> when preparation is not yet complete.

My servants are rebuked with a short reminder from My Spirit,
> when the tongues of My servants are victims of demonic slips."

Eze 45:4 "It shall be a holy *section* of the land, belonging to the priests, the ministers of the sanctuary, who come near to minister to the LORD; it shall be a place for their houses and a holy place for the sanctuary.
Divine Commentary—

"My servant is rebuked when his soul is still not under the control of his spirit.

My servant is rebuked at failure to heed the call to visit My prophet John.

My servant is rebuked when the input to his eyes;
> to his ears;
> carry the depravity of man,
> carry demonic content,
> carry the violence of man:
>> into the temple of My Spirit.

My servant is rebuked when unloving speech is directed at a spouse,
> at a child,
> at another saint of God.

My servant is rebuked when a soul in anger bubbles to the surface,
> when a soul in outburst becomes as a volcano spewing with great

                 ferment of intent,
    when a soul in rage spews profanity abroad.

My servant of rebuke may have a need for reparation,
       a need for apology for the attacking of the righteous,
       a need for forgiveness by his brothers for his deed
                 of shame.

My servant may have a need to stand in repentance before the assembly of God."

Eze 45:5 "*An area* twenty-five thousand *cubits* long and ten thousand wide shall belong to the Levites, the ministers of the temple; they shall have twenty chambers as a possession.
Divine Commentary—

"My servants are enthralled by the miracles of God,
      by the healings of God,
      by the wonders of God,
      by the signs of God.

My servants are attentive to the counsel of My Spirit,
   are attentive to the gifts of My Spirit,
   are attentive to the presence of My Spirit with a flaming torch.

My servants are receptive to The Will of God,
   are directed within The Will of God,
   are witnesses to the blessings issuing under The Will of God.

My servants are affirmed in their callings by My Spirit.

My servants are honoured by God,
      before the eyes of man,
      as they carry The Fear of God throughout The Earth."

Eze 45:6 "You shall appoint as the property of the city *an area* five thousand *cubits* wide and twenty-five thousand long, adjacent to the district of the holy *section;* it shall belong to the whole house of Israel.
Divine Commentary—

"My servants embrace their loving God,
   embrace the calls to praise,
   embrace the calls to worship,
   embrace the calls to prayer.

My servants embrace knowledge of their God.

My servants embrace The Wisdom of their God.

My servants embrace all they hold dear of their salvation:
      in hearts now reconciled with God."

Eze 45:7 "The prince shall have *a section* on one side and the other of the holy district and the city's property; and bordering on the holy district and the city's property, extending westward on the west side and eastward on the east side, the length *shall be* side by side with one of the *tribal* portions, from the west border to the east border.

Divine Commentary—

"My servants are the focus point of God.

My servants are the cynosure of My eyes.

My servants are the hope for the lost of God.

My servants are the blessed,
       are the honoured,
       are the highlights of the freewill of man."

My Content Study Aid

Divine Commentary— Ezekiel Ch 46

Eze 46:1 Thus says the Lord GOD: "The gateway of the inner court that faces toward the east shall be shut the six working days; but on the Sabbath it shall be opened, and on the day of the New Moon it shall be opened.
Divine Commentary—

"My servants observe the edicts of God.

My servants obey The Will of God.

My servants comply with the proclamations of God.

My servants wear the signs of the new covenant with Christ."

Eze 46:2 "The prince shall enter by way of the vestibule of the gateway from the outside, and stand by the gatepost. The priests shall prepare his burnt offering and his peace offerings. He shall worship at the threshold of the gate. Then he shall go out, but the gate shall not be shut until evening.
Divine Commentary—

"My servants live under the new covenant with Christ.

My servants experience the new covenant with Christ.

My servants endow with temples the new covenant with Christ.

My servants are the product of the new covenant with Christ."

Eze 46:3 "Likewise the people of the land shall worship at the entrance to this gateway before the LORD on the Sabbaths and the New Moons.
Divine Commentary—

"My servants are the examples of the new covenant with Christ.

My servants are the epitome of the new covenant with Christ.

My servants extend the new covenant with Christ.

My servants instruct in the new covenant with Christ."

Eze 46:4 "The burnt offering that the prince offers to the LORD on the Sabbath day *shall be* six lambs without blemish, and a ram without blemish;
Divine Commentary—

"My servants preach the new covenant with Christ.

My servants honour the new covenant with Christ.

My servants gather under the new covenant with Christ.

My servants worship in the new covenant with Christ."

Eze 46:5 "and the grain offering *shall be one* ephah for a ram, and the grain offering for the lambs, as much as he wants to give, as well as a hin of oil with every ephah.
Divine Commentary—

"My servants offer the new covenant with Christ.

My servants baptize for the new covenant with Christ.

My servants uphold the new covenant with Christ.

My servants declare the new covenant with Christ."

Eze 46:6 "On the day of the New Moon *it shall be* a young bull without blemish, six lambs, and a ram; they shall be without blemish.
Divine Commentary—

"My servants celebrate the new covenant with Christ.

My servants bring the new covenant with Christ.

My servants emphasize the new covenant with Christ.

My servants grow in the new covenant with Christ."

Eze 46:7 "He shall prepare a grain offering of an ephah for a bull, an ephah for a ram, as much as he wants to give for the lambs, and a hin of oil with every ephah.
Divine Commentary—

"My servants obtain wisdom within the new covenant with Christ.

My servants attend healings within the new covenant with Christ.

My servants witness miracles within the new covenant with Christ.

My servants bear testimonies of The Cross within the new covenant with Christ."

My Content Study Aid

Divine Commentary— Ezekiel Ch 47

Eze 47:1 Then he brought me back to the door of the temple; and there was water, flowing from under the threshold of the temple toward the east, for the front of the temple faced east; the water was flowing from under the right side of the temple, south of the altar.
Divine Commentary—

"My servants shield the weak and the elderly from the trials of the day,
        from inattention to their needs,
        from distancing from God.

My servants bring My gospel to a bedside,
    My gospel to the infirm and the dying,
    My gospel to the captives within the barred cages of man.

My servants fetch and carry,
    wash and clean,
    bathe and towel.

My servants bring companionship lacking from a life,
    bring kindness to a soul which once gave so much,
    bring a smiling face in greeting,
      a kiss upon a cheek,
      a handclasp of understanding—
        all which light a face."

Eze 47:2 He brought me out by way of the north gate, and led me around on the outside to the outer gateway that faces east; and there was water, running out on the right side.
Divine Commentary—

"My servants tend with care and love the mercy calls to the house-bound.

My servants visit the occupiers of the wheel chairs.

My servants bless and offer the ministry of God.

My servants sit down with strangers to My Church,
    sit down with those no longer able to make the trip,
    sit down to share the past,
    sit down to share the future in a relationship with God."

Eze 47:3 And when the man went out to the east with the line in his hand, he measured one thousand cubits, and he brought me through the waters; the water *came up to my ankles*.
Divine Commentary—

"My servants seek the hungry and the thirsty.

My servants bring fare from the table of The Lord.

My servants offer the fare for the soul,
>> the fare for the spirit,
>> the fare for the body.

My servants tell the story of a beginning with no end,
> tell the story filled with promises,
> tell the story of a new companion,
> tell the story of a journey and of the welcome home.

My servants tell the truth filled story of The Lord.

My servants know it is not too late to join in the seeking of their God as a disciple of The Lord."

Eze 47:4 Again he measured one thousand and brought me through the waters; the water *came up to my* knees. Again he measured one thousand and brought me through; the water *came up to my* waist.
Divine Commentary—

"My servants sing the songs of praise,
> sing the songs of worship,
> sing the songs of victory.

My servants sing the songs of the tongues of man.

My servants sing the songs of the angels in the heavens.

My servants sing the songs of childhood,
> sing the songs first learnt upon a mother's lap,
> sing the songs of choirs which carry to the heavens."

Eze 47:5 Again he measured one thousand, *and it was* a river that I could not cross; for the water was too deep, water in which one must swim, a river that could not be crossed.
Divine Commentary—

"My servants comfort and make cheery,
> teach and encourage,
> share and testify of God.

My servants raise The Faith level of the listener,
> increase interest by telling of their presence at the miracles of God,
> make available the word of God."

Eze 47:6 He said to me, "Son of man, have you seen *this?*" Then he brought me and returned me to the bank of the river.
Divine Commentary—

"My servants share the living water as it gushes for a life,
> watch as it converts a desert into an oasis all year round,
> are excited as Faith sprouts in its greenery—
>> as it covers the desolation of the sands,
> are jubilant at the change in the environment—

> where the heat of the desert is now cooled by the cascading
> of My Spirit.

My servants rejoice at where once there was no water to sprout the seed of Faith—
> yet now see the blooming of the garden of The Lord."

Eze 47:7 When I returned, there, along the bank of the river, *were* very many trees on one side and the other.

Divine Commentary—

"My servants clap their hands at the efforts of the gardener:
> where nothing bloomed before.

My servants clap their hands at the efforts of The Shepherd:
> to gather His sheep into the sheepfold
> before the onset of the night.

My servants clap their hands in love:
> to welcome souls into The Family of God."

My Content Study Aid

_____
_____
_____
_____
_____
_____
_____
_____
_____
_____
_____
_____
_____
_____
_____
_____
_____
_____
_____
_____

Divine Commentary— Ezekiel Ch 48

Eze 48:1 "Now these *are* the names of the tribes: From the northern border along the road to Hethlon at the entrance of Hamath, to Hazar Enan, the border of Damascus northward, in the direction of Hamath, *there shall be* one *section for* Dan from its east to its west side;
Divine Commentary—

"My servants validate the agency of their ministry with the leading of My Spirit,
   validate their agency through their sincerity in prayer,
   validate their agency with the evidence of their Faith.

 The God who calls My servants has no difficulty in establishing the truth."

Eze 48:2 "by the border of Dan, from the east side to the west, one *section for* Asher;
Divine Commentary—

"My servants need not fear a slip,
   need not fear an oversight,
   need not fear a document mislaid.

My servants are surrounded by the 'Abba' of the nation,
   by the 'Abba' of The Family of God,
   by the 'Abba' who knows His children very well."

Eze 48:3 "by the border of Asher, from the east side to the west, one *section for* Naphtali;
Divine Commentary—

"My servants need not scurry as a slave,
   need not be ready to hurdle fences,
   need not be ready to dash and serve,
   need not be ready to drop and run.

My servants need to know the urgency of man is not the urgency of God."

Eze 48:4 "by the border of Naphtali, from the east side to the west, one *section for* Manasseh;
Divine Commentary—

"My servants exercise My ministry within their borders set by God.

My servants should not stray to that for which they are not charged.

My servants do not have authority to exceed The Will of God.

My servants do not carry My ministry:
   when outside the envelope of My Spirit—
      where He has not gone before.

My servants cannot force My Spirit to go before:
   when He has not been released by God.

My servants should not make assumptions as to the extent of their mantles of
>> My ministry:
>>> when they rush and do not tarry before The Lord."

Eze 48:5 "by the border of Manasseh, from the east side to the west, one *section for* Ephraim;
Divine Commentary—

"My servants are not immune to the interference of man:
> to man at his worst—
>> yet within his own freewill.

My servants should use wisdom:
> when confronted by man within his wardrobe of authority.

My servants put their lives at risk:
> when they do not listen to the screamers and the wielders of the
>> weapons of the day.

My servants should wipe their feet to move to where My Spirit counsels,
> to where My Spirit has prepared.

My servants should not attempt to minister:
> where man has slammed the door to that which he controls.

My servants should not stay:
> where they are not welcome in this end-time of the harvest."

Eze 48:6 "by the border of Ephraim, from the east side to the west, one *section for* Reuben;
Divine Commentary—

"My servants do not need to scrape and bow before the agency of man,
> should not imprint the authority of God upon the potentate of man,
> should not antagonize the angry in defiance of the demons.

My servants enquire of My Spirit in determining the time and place:
> to stand in confrontation against satanic forces.

My servants should never be alone,
> as the only soul,
>> when in the front line of the battlefield of God."

Eze 48:7 "by the border of Reuben, from the east side to the west, one *section for* Judah;
Divine Commentary—

"My servants are the Victors of Revelation,
> are the Drummers of the Cross,
> are the Passers of the Faith.

My servants are the Holders of the Expertise,
> are the Equipped by God,

are the Spikers of the Devil's guns.

My servants are My chosen envoys for The End-time gathering of My souls.

And The Father said,
'Amen.' "

My Content Study Aid

Appendix

Journaling and Notes (1)	246
Journaling and Notes (2)	247
Journaling and Notes (3)	248
About the Scribe	249

Book One (3) Reviews
    1st Reviewer: GB   250
    2nd Reviewer: AJE   250
    3rd Reviewer: DN   250

Book Four (3) Reviews
    1st Reviewer: RM   252
    2nd Reviewer: AG   253
    3rd Reviewer: SGS   253

Journaling and Notes (1)

Journaling and Notes (2)

Journaling and Notes (3)

About The Scribe

Updated 18 February 2019

Anthony is 78, having been married to his wife, Adrienne, for 55 years. They have five married children: Carolyn, Alan, Marie, Emma and Sarah and fourteen grandchildren: Matthew & Ella; Phillipa & Jonathan; Jeremy, Ngaire & Trevor; Jake, Finn, Crystal & Caleb; Bjorn, Greta & Minka.

Anthony was raised on a dairy farm in Springston, Canterbury, NZ in the 1940s. He graduated from Canterbury University, Christchurch, NZ with a B.Sc. in chemistry and mathematics in 1962. He was initially employed as an industrial chemist in flour milling and linear programming applications.

These used the first IBM 360 at the university for determining least cost stock food formulations and production parameters. Later he was involved in similar applications on the refining side of the oil industry in Britain, Australia and New Zealand. This was followed by sales and managerial experience in the chemical industry.

The family moved to a Bay of Plenty, NZ, town in 1976 when Anthony took up funeral directing, as a principal, expanding an initial sibling partnership until the close of the century. Anthony acquired practical experience in accounting, business management, and computer usage (early Apples— including The Lisa).

Upon retiring from active funeral directing in 2000 and selling his interests, he then commenced the promotion and the writing of funeral management software for the NZ funeral environment. Rewarded with national success, he has now retired, in 2007, from the active management of that interest, living near some of his family in Hamilton NZ.

Anthony was brought up in the Methodism of his father until his mid-teens, his mother's side was Open Brethren. He is Christian in belief within an Apostolic Pentecostal Charismatic framework of choice (since the 1990s) having been earlier in the Mormon church for several years. Thereafter he was in the Baptist denomination followed by finding a home within the Acts (Apostolic) church movement for some years, and now in Glory Release Ministries, one where all have made him welcome.

He and his wife, who has visited a number of Asian countries, have been to India in 2011, 12, 13, 16 and 18 on The Lord's tasks and have witnessed and participated in many miracles which befall His people and the multitudes.

His forbears William Henry Eddy and Margaret Jane Eddy, née Oats, emigrated to New Zealand from Gulval, Cornwall, England in 1878 on a sailing ship, with a very slow passage time of 79 days, and with their three month old infant child, Margaret Anne, dying 21 October 1878 from Congestion of the brain on board the Marlborough while en route to NZ. The Marlborough sailed London 19 September 1878, via Plymouth 26 September 1878, and arrived Lyttelton 14 December 1878 with 336 assisted immigrants. His grandfather, Alfred Charles Eddy, then but three years old, together with an older brother aged four, obviously survived the trials of the sea voyage to become a part of a family with a further eleven New Zealand born siblings all living to maturity.

Book 1 (3) Reviews

Of Book 1 — Three people are saying:

'GOD Speaks of Return and Bannered'

1st Reviewer: GB

'GOD SPEAKS of Return and Bannered' is a fascinating collection of divinely originated texts transcribed from the visionary voice of God, exhorting those with eyes to see and ears to listen, to unite under the Kingdom Flag (Emblem) of God and to prepare for the second coming. With strong references to biblical passages containing guidance to this effect, this book will be a spiritually uplifting study vehicle for all who seek spiritual enlightenment through Pentecostal teachings.

2nd Reviewer: AJE

This is where it all began: The very first collection in Anthony Eddy's "God Speaks" series of poetry. This is the very beginning of fictional prophet Anthony Eddy's communion with the Lord and transmission of His missives from above. In this book, God announces His return to the world of man and reiterates the messages present in the Biblical scriptures: Man's fall, damnation, and salvation at His hands.
Although a bit more fire-and-brimstone oriented than later works in the series, "GOD SPEAKS of Return and Bannered" is still a must-have for any believer's ebook library. The messages of salvation and inspiration presented herein are spectacularly written. They absolutely should not go to waste. My one nitpick is that the nature of Eddy's prophethood is never explicitly stated to be a fictional trapping for the poems presented; however, I don't really think that's a big deal, since it's clear from a close reading of the text. A+, I highly recommend.

3rd Reviewer: JD

I had actually read the other two books in this series before I read this one. I wasn't aware of the chronology of the books, and I would've started with this one if I had my time back. "GOD Speaks of Return and Bannered" is the first book of a series that talks about God's will, including that of mankind and the book also imparts wisdom in addition to explanations of prophecies particularly with regards to that of the second coming.
It makes use of references from the Bible. I must say that I thoroughly enjoyed the section of the History of the Book, as it basically paves the way or explain how this book came to be. I also enjoyed all the images contained herein, as the other books didn't really have pictures and I find that pictures somewhat keeps the audience attention a bit more.
As with the other books, I like the poetry style, even though this whole book isn't written in that manner it still contains a fair bit of it. I also like the direct scriptural references and

it will be good too for those who want to check what the Bible has to say about it. The section describing the flag is also nice. It gives the reader a history or maybe even an understanding of what it is about. I also appreciate the information about the author and a bit of his family history. Overall I enjoyed all the books in the series even though as I have said before I am not a religious person!

Book 4 (3) Reviews

Of Book 4 — Three people are saying:

'God Speaks To Man in The End-time'

1st Reviewer: RM

This is quite an intriguing book. It is not like the traditional stories with characters and a story line. It is different. In terms of contents, it is great, full of warnings about many different subjects, all related to how God expect us to behave in different contexts. The format is different of what you would expect from a traditional writing. It remind me poetry style, but with some special particularities. This is a book that you do not read in one sit, but read a topic per day, savoring its message. And although the format might be difficult to read, the message is crystal clear. We should stay away from sin and be prepared for the return of Christ at the end of times, keeping our faith strong.
At the introduction he claims that the calls he describe in the book are not of his own writing, but should have the words "And I hear The Lord Jesus saying..." denoting that part of the text is of a Divine origin. The author divides the topics (or calls) he addresses mostly in two pages sections for a total of 56 calls, like "Surroundings of Man", "Purity of My Bride", "Lack of Faith", "My People", etc.
I recommend this book to all Christians that wants a boost of confidence that they are in the correct path for their salvation. The author shares his views and his solid faith and we should praise him for that! I would give this book a 3.5 to 4 stars (out of 5) and I would not mind at all paying for this book something up to US$ 4.99.
Inkspand.com was kind enough to provide this book for me for reviewing and I was not requested to provide a positive review. Opinions expressed here are my own.

Book 4 'God Speaks To Man in The End-time'

2nd Reviewer: AG

From the point of view of a non-religious reader, the format is a bit perplexing, but the content is refreshing. This isn't a straight-up religious reading, this isn't forcing religion down your throat. This is giving you an interesting way to read through someone else's eyes, this is giving you insight. I chose to read this book because I am not personally religious, and have always found religion something I personally do not choose to devote my life to. Reading from the point of view of someone who does choose to devote their life to faith is far more interesting than I had expected. This gives you pros and cons of your actions, warnings of the future and how your actions may affect you. It warns humanity of its loss of faith, of how its meandering through life deviates from God's views. In a way, this book teaches us not that religion is absolute, but that humanity is absolute, and to treat each other in ways that God has not foretold or suggested is to deny our very humanity itself. It warns us of sin, it congratulates us on things done according to the lord. This book could be classified as self-help from a religious standpoint. Again, from the point of view of someone who doesn't share the author's faith, this is an extremely interesting read. Anthony speaks from his heart and his faith, and his faith is strong. He truly believes in the ways of his religion and in that way he wishes to share his faith, and share his humanity.

3rd Reviewer: SGS

God Speaks to Man in The End-time by Anthony A. Eddy is a very interesting book, it's almost like the Bible. You may call it the author's version of The Bible. Editing is sort of perfect, with almost no grammatical or punctuation errors. Although there is no plot, no characters, I like the way the book has been written.
It is, however, appealing to only those of us who are very strong believers. Most of the people don't have enough patience to sit through the book or the depth of philosophy to understand it. The writer is professing his beliefs through the book, hence, the readers form a narrow group, so I'll have o be watchful while recommending it, since you can't tell everyone to go and check it out.
The format is unique, and content is inspiring. It gives you superb insights, a new way to see things. As I said earlier, for a person who is religious, the book is awesome. But for a non believer or a not so strong believer, the book holds low charms.
The book teaches us not that religion is as important as humanity, and that we should treat each other in ways that the lord wants us to. The book is almost a self help, and an inspiration, but from a religious standpoint.
The style of poems is unique and charming. It feels as if God Himself is talking to you. That's the part I loved the most about the book.
Good luck!

www.ingramcontent.com/pod-product-compliance
Lightning Source LLC
Chambersburg PA
CBHW071305110526
44591CB00010B/786